WHEN A MAN LOVES A WOMAN | PATRICK AUGUSTUS

The
X
Press

Published in United Kingdom by:
The X Press,
6 Hoxton Square, London N1 6NU
Tel: 0171 729 1199
Fax: 0171 729 1771

This edition published in 1998

Printed by Caledonian Book Manufacturing, Glasgow, Scotland.

Distributed in UK by Turnaround Distribution, Unit 3, Olympia Trading Estate,
Coburg Road, London N22 6TZ
Tel: 0181 829 3000
Fax: 0181 881 5088

ISBN 1-874509-24-7

ABOUT THE AUTHOR

Born in south London of Jamaican parents, Patrick Augustus has worked for many years as a musician and record producer. As well as being the author of four novels, he has written and directed several plays, is a regular radio contributor, and is a founder member of *The Baby Fathers Alliance*, a pressure group for separated fathers. Aged 33, Augustus is currently living in Tenerife in the Canary Islands, where he is writing his next novel.

Yaowza! Before I begin this uplifting story, I just want to give a strong shout to all the positive brothas and sistas out there. You know who you are, and you know who you ain't.
Patrick Augustus, Ten-a-grief, 1998

<u>BOOK I</u>

CAMPBELL'S STORY

The best thing that happened to me was when I learned to say 'no'.
Men don't believe they can say 'no'. I didn't believe it either. But
I'm different now. Like most of the fellas I spar with, I used to be
like, "no way can you say 'no' to a woman who hands it to you on
a plate—butt naked and all, no strings attached..." Even with
strings attached—hell, it's only string! I just couldn't say 'no'. No
mountain high nor river deep could keep me away from some hot
sex. Even if it was on the other side of the world, you'd find me
there. That's how I got involved with Theresa in the first place. She
was twenty-five, and worked as a cashier at a bank in east London,
Hackney, to be precise. She always had a big smile on her face,
which seemed to widen every time I came in to cash a cheque. Two-
twos we started exchanging pleasantries and before I knew it she
was saying, in her chatty mix of northern accent and Jamaican
patois, that she had a couple of tickets for a comedy show at the
local Empire Theatre, and I was saying I was free all evening.
Free? Ain't nothing free in this world and with Terri, I was paying
my dues 'til way past dawn. Now don't get me wrong, I don't see
nothing wrong with a little after hours bump and grind. But
why's it always gotta be all or nothing? The last thing I was
thinking about while putting on the performance of a lifetime was
that she was thinking, 'Mmmn, dis t'ing yah so sweet me haffe
control it.'

Giving her too much sweetness on that night was my first
mistake. I shoulda just done the nasty one time, or maybe twice,
but no, she wanted me to show her every move I knew and so I had

1

to try it this way and that way and this and that way. And even when I was just about to fall asleep at daybreak, with the birds singing away outside, all she could say was, "Five times is alright, but a woman can keep having orgasms all night and day." That should have been warning enough for me to stay away from this one, but instead I took it like a slap in the face of my macho ego and took up the challenge. Next time, I promised myself...next time I was gonna give this woman such sweet agony that she'd be tearing her hair out.

Well, it didn't end with the next time. Nor the next. I was at Terri's place night after night after night. And it was like nothing, I mean nothing I did could satisfy her. Eventually she said I might as well move into her flat seeing as I was spending most of my time there anyway.

That was my second mistake. It seemed like a good idea at the time, especially as I was tired of living in a damp basement flat on Amhurst Road with rip-off rent and crackheads pissing on my doorstep. Her little place on the Marshes had all the creature comforts—central heating, wall to wall carpeting, IKEA furniture and a widescreen television with cable...I had only known the woman two weeks and already I was carrying my stereo and my entire collection of Studio One records up to her third floor flat.

Anyway, things were sweet for the first coupla months. All we did when she came home from work every evening, was have sex. We'd start at 6pm and stop for dinner around 8pm. Then we'd start again and carry on well into the night. And not no ordinary sex neither, but some wild, loud and intense stuff. I was determined to satisfy this woman, or die trying.

I don't know how she managed to get up for work in the mornings. I was alright the first coupla days, and somehow managed to drag myself in. But after that it was like, 'I gotta sleep...I need my sleep!' Before I knew it, I hadn't been to work for a month and by the time I decided to go in, there wasn't a job waiting for me. When I told her, Terri was like, "So what? Sales jobs are easy to get, Campbell. We can manage on my wages 'til you find something else." It was an offer I couldn't refuse, so I kicked back to catch up on some daytime television and started hanging out at the gym regularly because by now it was looking like I needed to build up my stamina for the evening workout.

After six months of the wickedest slam, I had to accept that I was never gonna satisfy her, so there was no use trying. I settled down to a normal sex life with Terri and started hanging out more with the fellas to reclaim my nights.

Now why do sistas have to read something into every little thing a brotha does? Terri wasn't into no rationing business and wanted to know why I wasn't giving her all the loving she needed. I wasn't going to tell her that she had me beat, so she concluded that it had to be another woman and that she hoped that I was using a condom. I assured her that there was no other woman — that I just wanted to take things easy for a while. I made a joke about it being my time of the month, which she didn't find funny, and then I put an arm around her, looked deep into her eyes, kissed her gently on the nose, on her forehead, on her neck and before long, we were on the living room floor, tearing each other's clothes off and giving each other the loving that we both wanted.

Looking back, that was another mistake. Why was I explaining everything to her? You see, as far as I'm concerned at this point, we're lovers, nothing more. We're not an item or anything. Sure, we're living together, or rather I'm crashing at her crib, but I don't see any ring on my finger and I don't remember any promises either. Sure, we're living on her money, but I keep the flat clean and tidy…that's the deal. Suddenly, I find myself having to give the who, what, where and why and I start thinking, 'this is how it's gonna be for the rest of your life if you don't find your own place soon'.

Terri was probably reading my thoughts, because after that day there was no more talk of the 'other' woman or how 'few' times we were having sex. Instead it was all milk and honey for the next six months.

But what I thought was milk and honey, was in fact scheming.

Six months of scheming. It started out with little things. She would come home early from work and make me a meal out of her Caribbean cookbook, or she'd take me shopping because she had seen an outfit that would look great on me. Then she always managed to get two tickets to a show somewhere on the weekend. And on pay day, she'd come home with a little present for me. Always something gold. A bracelet, a necklace, a fountain pen. Don't ask me how she got the money for it. She said it was savings, in which case the Cartier watch she got me must have gone quite some way to wiping her out.

I didn't ask her for that watch and didn't feel good about it. But she refused to take it back.

My final mistake. I had only worn it a week, when she hit me with the payback as we were in the middle of another late night passionate embrace.

"Campbell, is this just a grind or what?" she asked suddenly.

Coming out of the blue as it did, I didn't know what to say, but I saw a minefield ahead.

"So, it's just a grind…" Terri echoed my thoughts, not my words, with a tone and a look in her eyes that told me she knew the truth. But still I didn't shift my position. I just looked down at her with a blank expression, still moving slowly inside her. She folded her arms around her bare breasts and looked away with a sour pout of her lips.

By the time I got up the next morning, she had already packed my bag and boxed my records. She wanted me out. She even took the day off work to make sure that I took my troubles somewhere else—away from her.

All I could think about was that I should have got my act together a lot quicker and got somewhere to live. I should have, I should have, I should have, but I didn't…I gave her back the necklace and the bracelet and the fountain pen and the Cartier watch. I didn't want to owe her anything. She took them back without hesitation as if she was expecting them back anyway. I got dressed, still trying to figure out where I was going to spend the night. A list of names and faces ran through my mind. I took the Adidas bag with my things in and told her I'd have to come back for the records.

I went up the road to the call box and flicked through my address book. Called number after number. But twelve months is a long time to be out of circulation and man an' man's circumstances had changed. Some people were like, "Campbell who?" So much for the homies...

I stayed in a hotel in Finsbury Park for the first coupla nights, lying in bed listening to the hoes until dawn and spending the days running through the rest of the numbers in my book. I still didn't get anywhere. My final port of call, as always, was Trevor's house. Trevor's my long-time spar, he's always been there for me. If I wasn't desperate I wouldn't have turned to him, because I knew how things were tight for him also. All he had was a tiny bedsit in Holloway. And what's more he had a child somewhere to support.

So I go back to Terri's to get my box of records and she's gone. Her flat is completely empty. I mean empty. The TV's gone, the IKEA furniture's gone. Even the wall to wall carpeting has been spirited away. And of course, there's no sign of my records.

At the bank, they said that she had handed in her notice two days before and had moved back to her family home in Manchester. No, they didn't have any forwarding address for her.

So there I was without a home, without a job and having to listen to the familiar scratches of my records every time a pirate deejay dropped a Studio One selection! In twelve months, I had lost the little that I had and every night when I went home to sleep on Trevor's floor, I would think of Terri and how she taught me to say 'no'.

And that's what women can't understand. They'll be like, "Yeah right! Show me a man prepared to turn down some free pussy and I'll show you a dyam liar!"

According to a recent survey, 54% of black men would rather end their relationships than perform oral sex on their partners. 44% would try their best to talk their women out of it. Only 2% were prepared to admit that they not only performed oral sex regularly, but also enjoyed it.

ONCE UPON A TIME

The sauna was steaming. The temperature dial was at 110 and inching upwards. The middle-aged white dude shifted his naked body, scratching uncomfortably and letting out a groan of misery. He got up hurriedly to leave.

"Hot enough for you, then?" he asked, with more than a hint of irony.

Sitting cross-legged opposite each other on the top benches, with only a towel around their waists, Trevor and Campbell exchanged a grinning glance.

"Au contraire, my good man," Trevor replied, "it's not hot enough."

The white dude shook his head doubtfully and pushed his way out.

Three afternoons a week at the Holloway Road pool was for the brothas. Up until midday, it was mostly pensioners and swimmers, but from about 2pm when the entrance fee was halved, the place got taken over by the Black Men United crew. Black Men United weren't a football team or anything quite so structured. They were just a loose collection of guys who happened to meet every week for a steam bath. But they were like an extended family. A random mix of men from seventeen to seventy whom Campbell could train, laugh and reason with. Usually they would work out for an hour or two in the gym, sometimes together and sometimes individually, depending on who was there on time and who was steppin' to BMT. And then

7

they'd make their way to the sauna and that's when things got really hot.

It wasn't like they excluded anybody either. Anyone else was welcome, but when you put a whole bunch of black guys together in a sauna, they start behaving like they are in Africa or in the Caribbean or anywhere where the climate's sultry and the laughter's loud. Somehow, nobody else wanted to be around when Black Men United took over the sauna and it was an unspoken rule that Tuesday, Thursday and Sunday afternoons were 'black man time'. Right through until closing time, you would find youths there who had come to skylark and others who were there to reason about all manner of t'ing an' t'ing, especially how to make some extra digits. And of course there were the same old arguments about women.

"I mean me and women…it always gets screwed up somehow. It always starts out fine. You know how it is when you first meet a woman and everything's just fresh and you think she's the perfect this or that and you really work hard at chasing them and call them up every day and you'd see them any chance you got…and then after a while, you get to know them…and hey presto you come crashing down to earth with a thump. I mean, it's nothing but pain every time…"

Trevor grinned. This wasn't the first time he had heard Campbell distressed about women and he was sure that it wouldn't be the last. Although he denied it, Campbell loved to talk about women. Even though he made out that it bugged him so bad to even think about them, he couldn't do without them. As his friend, Trevor felt that he knew him well enough to know what he needed.

"Networking. That's what it's all about nowadays. You ain't getting nowhere the way you're going so you might as well give it a try. Everybody's doing it. If you wanna meet a woman —a single black woman—the right single black woman—you go to a networking club. Simple. Hook yourself up, man. You'll thank me for it, believe!"

"Trevor man, you've got to understand, I don't want a woman, I don't need a woman. I'm kinda getting used to living without 'em. You ought to try it some time."

"Me? You're crazy! I've done that...eighteen months, remember? I ain't doing that again."

Yeah, Campbell remembered. But that wasn't the same thing. That was at 'Her Majesty's leisure'. He was talking voluntary.

"It's good for the soul, y'know. Now I know what Marvin Gaye was talking about. 'Sexual healing' is when you stay away from women. Every man should try it."

"I'd like to see you tell that to any of those guys over at the Scrubs, or in Brixton, or up in Pentonville," Trevor laughed.

When you saw him out on the streets, dressed in his immaculate two-piece, his hair neatly trimmed and wheeling and dealing, it was easy to forget about the time he had done. Fraud wasn't a real crime, after all. Especially when it only involved signing a few papers and ending up with mortgages on twelve properties which you intended eventually to rent at a profit. Trevor was a juggler who survived by giving a good impression, and as several mortgage companies had learned to their cost, he certainly looked as if he should own several houses.

"If you can't do the crime..." Campbell said.

"Sure you can do the time...that ain't the problem. But can you live without a woman? Now that's a whole different kinda time. I'm telling you, when you're inside, all you're thinking about is your woman...counting the days until you get released and thinking that the first thing you're gonna do when you come out is lock yourself in a room with her for the next month. Why do you think people do so much exercise when they're inside? It's 'cause they know their

9

woman isn't going to be too happy after waiting all that time if her man comes out with a tired, lazy body."

"Okay, so I guess sex is overrated when you're inside?"

"It isn't just about sex. When you're locked up with a bunch of guys for eighteen months, you just want to be able to touch a woman again, smell a woman…talk to a woman. What do you think all those page 3 girls are doing stuck up on the walls? It's just in case you've forgotten what a woman looks like."

"I'm not that desperate," Campbell laughed.

But Trevor wasn't finished yet. He continued seriously in a low voice, just above a whisper, as if he was telling his spar the world's greatest secret, something he shouldn't breathe a word about. "Being without a woman for a long stretch does funny things to a man, believe. I've seen man an' man with their heads messed up. Even most of these big man you see out on street, walking like they're bad bwoys and telling everybody that they're ruffnecks. What do you think they do when they've been inside for a few years without a woman? I'm telling you, man. That's why I get worried when you tell me all this 'living without a woman' stuff. I've seen man hug up man, y'know, just because he couldn't find a woman."

"Don't overdo it, Trevor, all I said was that I was taking a break from women. Doesn't mean I'm giving up women for good."

"But what is the point? Why? You said that it didn't bother you. You said that Terri didn't mean a thing to you. You're acting like this was the first time a woman ever threw you out. It's happened once before, remember? Or have you forgotten what's her name, the gal with the big gap in her teeth?"

No, Campbell hadn't forgotten.

"Jenny."

"Jenny, Terri…what's the difference?"

To Trevor, there was no difference. A woman was a woman. But to Campbell, every woman carried her own particular bag of mystery. Jenny was enjoyable to be with— a woman who never tired of telling stories and remembering the funny things that had happened in her nonstop, no-turning-back life. Sometimes she used to talk so much she rarely finished one sentence before taking off on another. They had a good thing going for a while and if her childhood sweetheart hadn't returned suddenly after four years on a world tour, she probably wouldn't have thrown him out. Terri, on the other hand, was a whole other experience—totally unpredictable. The only thing you could expect from her was the unexpected. She talked less, but had a mind that raced ahead of her body. She didn't know what she was going to do from one minute to the next and didn't want to know, preferring to change her mind rapidly enough to say 'yes' one day and 'no' the very next. Once her mind started ticking, the wheels just kept turning, no matter how much you tried to stop them.

"The difference is two years and a whole lot more besides."

"Two years already...Do you remember how you got over it?"

"Yes, I remember."

"Tenerife...Club 18-30...you bonked your way out of love that time!" Trevor chuckled. "Do you remember how good you felt when we got back? You couldn't even remember who Jenny was."

Yes, Campbell remembered that also.

"Hey, maybe we can get get a cheap flight. Go again."

"I'm thirty-one now," Campbell reminded him. "Club 18-30 won't have me, I'm too old. "

"Seriously man, we could go off somewhere together...I haven't had a holiday in a while. We could kick back, relax and meet some women."

"Seriously Trevor, I'm not interested in a bonking holiday. Besides I'm busted, remember. I ain't got no papers."

"Leave that to me. Pay me back when you're ready."

"Man, thanks but no…"

Campbell was embarrassed. He owed his spar enough already. Campbell knew his priorities and knew he had to start paying his friend back before thinking of going on holiday anywhere. Especially when money was this tight to mention.

"Man, this ain't a psychological thing is it?" Trevor asked as an afterthought. "I mean, you haven't forgotten how to check woman or anything like that?"

Campbell slapped him playfully and told him to behave himself.

"And you're not afraid of women either?"

Campbell warned his friend again.

"Then why don't you just come along to this networking club on Saturday anyway? Nobody's forcing you to check woman, but you never know, you might see a honey that you like. If you don't, we can still have a laugh."

Campbell nodded half-heartedly. He suspected that his friend just didn't want to go by himself. Either way, it didn't look like he was going to get out of this one. So he agreed.

"And make sure you bring some boxing gloves, 'cause the gals dem gwine mad over you," Trevor laughed.

With that settled, Trevor folded his legs in the lotus position and reverted back to his meditation, his eyes closed, his breathing steadily controlled.

In one way it was nice for Campbell to hear all this concern for his well-being from his main spar. One of the few times men ever show any closeness to each other is when one of their friends has been dumped by his woman. In the last few weeks, Trevor had been really supportive and, assuming that Campbell must be desperate for it, was going out of his way to introduce him to women or to take him to places where he could meet them. He had even gone so far as to arrange blind dates for his spar and to invite him to a dinner, the sole intention of which was to invite a single woman for him to 'view'. And no matter how many times Campbell told him that he'd learned to say 'no', Trevor always replied by saying he was one of those guys who didn't take 'no' for an answer.

The twins entered the sauna, towels wrapped around each of their bodybuilding bodies.

"So wha'ppen, old man?" one of them asked. "You trying to cold up the place?"

Campbell looked up at the two and grinned. He pointed to the hot stove in the centre of the room and said, "Be my guest."

"Sweet," said the twin, flashing a 24-carat smile, and proceeded to mix a few drops of olbas oil into some water from the bucket beside the stove, before splashing it over the hot coals. The steam rose to the ceiling in a whooosh.

It was definitely hot enough now, even for the twins who were forced to sit on the bench on the lower level where it was cooler. Campbell didn't know the twins by their proper names, other than that one was Ruffy and the other was Tuffy and that they worked as bouncers at a night club several times a week. He knew a few of Black Men United by their given names, but most people used a nickname. Real names weren't important when you got on so well.

The 'collective' was so informal that you didn't even know where most of them lived or what they did to make a living, or whether they were married or had kids or where they went after the sauna. Yet, since discovering the thrice weekly sessions, Campbell wouldn't miss a day if he could help it.

This was how he found out about what was blowing up and who was livin' large and who was recording with whom and which raves were the ones to attend at the weekend. They were 'brothas' who shared in each other's ups and downs and tried to save each other the tears. There was actually something quite appealing about this kind of relationship, where everything was bullshit free. When you came to the sauna, you hung your ego in the changing rooms.

"Everybody said it couldn't happen," Ruffy was telling his brother, "that you couldn't get a million black men together on the same spot, but it happened, and I'm telling you it was one of the most beautiful things I've ever seen, man. You shoulda been there, bro."

Close on their heels came Sweetbwoy, a half-Indian, half-black youth in his early twenties, who had a pretty face and defiant dark brown nipples sprouting out of the velvety chocolate skin covering his muscular chest. A seasoned flirt, Sweetbwoy had all the luck when it came to ladies and dared any woman to resist his charms. He had turned lovemaking into an art, he claimed, and could seduce any woman he wanted and was reputed to currently have a whole bunch of women 'powdering' him, one or two of whom were wealthy enough to keep him in Armani suits and Calvin Klein underwear. It was even rumoured that Sweetbwoy made a living as a call boy. All a woman had to do was page him, arrange a date, and he would arrive on her doorstep with a bunch of flowers.

"Ooooooh yeeees...the casanova is in the place y'all...and he's looking good y'all...looks like he's gonna get a little something tonight y'all...a'rrriiight!!" Tuffy broke into a crotch-grabbing rap.

Sweetbwoy smiled at his friend and thanked him for the introduction, while confirming theatrically that tonight was indeed going to be "one of those nights".

"You know me...always in the chill mood...I'll be kickin' back with a couple of honeys...crazy sexy honeys. You know the type; honeys who expect the very best in good loving and settle for nothing less. Two very horny ladies, gentlemen, my most exciting sexual conquests…taking care of me all night. Let it be known that Angela is official and she's gonna take care of my top half while Althea gets the honour of taking care of my bottom half…be warned, if you live in the Holloway Road area, there will be bawling, screaming, loud moaning and some hard grinding tonight."

By now, the twins were cheering their spar on with ecstatic whoops of approval.

A longtime regular named Freddy had arrived quietly and squeezed his way in between the twins. He was fat, very fat, and upon arriving would always take up a considerable amount of bench space in the cubicle, despite the protestations of some of the slimmer occupants. Freddy wasn't a big talker, at least until he got to know you. But when he was among friends, Freddy was unsilenceable. He had a lot to say and would get involved with any of the conversations going on and get on anybody's case if he had to. Today his comments were directed at Sweetbwoy.

"Yaow coolie bwoy, wha' de blouse an' skirt you know 'bout giving a gal what she want? Cho', you too maaga?"

For some reason both of the twins thought that was one of the funniest things they had ever heard and fell about the cubicle cracking up with hysterical laughter.

"Hear him nuh!" Ruffy roared.

Sweetbwoy was unphased. He was used to being teased as well as boosted.

"You talking to me, Fat Freddy? I suppose you're gonna tell us now that the ladies prefer someone like you—an overweight lover?"

"I ain't overweight. You might call me overweight 'cause you're too damn maaga, but, I ain't down with that. This is pure muscle, man…"

Again there were hoots of laughter from the others.

"Man, rice and peas and exercise built this body," Freddy insisted.

"I think you overdid it with the peas there Fat Man. They said a plateful not a potful."

"Y'nah'mean?" Freddy nodded. "You're just jealous 'cause maaga man caan do not'n fe gal pickney. Skeen? Ah strictly big belly man the nowadays gal ah bawl fe. Making love ain't about what you've got on the outside, man. You see me, you might call me tubby on the outside, but underneath I'm a tiger. They don't call me 'big' for not'n. Skinny or fat, light-skinned or black, it doesn't bother me, I'll take 'em and make love to 'em for days on end. Skeen? Dat's why the gal dem love me and call me big pappa, the condom filler…You nuh see't? Me jus' love dem style deh."

"Yeah yeah yeah," Sweetbwoy said dismissively.

"Y'see, the woman nowadays ain't interested in no quick slim t'ing, 'cause unuh don't know how to use the little you got. She wants to be made love to slowly. All dat Speedy Gonzales business done long time. A heavyweight breddah like me is built for comfort, not for speed. And the woman nowadays need that comfort to express dem full repertoire. Skeen?"

No, Sweetbwoy didn't see it. But Freddy wasn't giving up and he was appealing in vain for support among those in the now packed cubicle.

"Maaga man nuh know 'bout real love making…about treating a woman like a delicate flower or a succulent mango. You see me, I've got the good dick. You nevah know? Makes the women drop their drawers slowly. I can bring a woman to orgasm with just one kiss. Wait until you get to my size, that's when the women love to cuddle you like dem cuddle teddy bear. That's what they call sensuality. Skeen? 'Nuff woman ah complain up an' down 'bout how dem too fed up with all ah unuh skinny guys 'cause you don't have dat sint'ing deh."

16

The conversation continued like that into the evening, with people coming and going and some dipping in and out of the steam bath beside it. Campbell stayed in for a long, long stint because it helped him relax and because Thursdays at the sauna was the cheapest live entertainment you could get anywhere in London. There was always something new to hear and you always went home on a high.

"Hey Sweetbwoy, you know who Freddy looks like?" Tuffy announced loudly as they were changing back to their street clothes afterwards.

Freddy saw it coming and braced himself for the inevitable diss.

"Oprah with a receding hairline!"

Everybody cracked up with laughter and most people agreed that there was something in it. Freddy simply grinned. A gold cap beaming from his mouth.

84% of black men who are currently sexually active are confident they can let their partner know what they want to happen. 9% aren't sure and 7% say they can't.

TWO TO TANGO

Campbell and Trevor got ready together for the evening's reverie. They were going out to the Ebony Club networking ball down at one of the posh hotels on Park Lane. Earlier in the day, Campbell had swung by Moss Bros on Regent Street, in between passengers, to pick up two dinner suits from their hire department, one for him and one for his spar. By the time they had freshened up with a shower, coiffed their hair and donned their suits, they both looked sharp. Campbell took some polish and gave his and Trevor's shoes a shine to add the finishing touch. They admired each other and said "Crissas!" before leaving the bedsit.

They drove down in the Jag to arrive in style, which was just as well because everywhere you looked in the back streets behind the hotel were pure Benzos, Porsches and BMWs parked up. They locked the car and made their way casually as if they weren't phased by anything, like they were used to dressing in style and like they had a million in offshore bank accounts.

"You should count yourself lucky that you're working," Trevor insisted when Campbell complained that he felt like Morgan Freeman in *Driving Miss Daisy*. "Jah know what I had to go through to hook you up in the first place."

Campbell did count himself lucky and was grateful to Trevor for recommending him. That was what spars were for, and the two had been tight since their junior school days. What was more, he could imagine what the scheming

19

Trevor had to go through to convince Louie, the owner, to employ him as the only black driver at Xecutive Cars. Louie had made it clear to him from the first day that he was on probation and that if the company's customers didn't take to a "touch of colour" in their drivers, he'd have to reconsider. 'And you can kiss my battyhole', Campbell thought, but didn't say. He needed this job desperately. He had even bought a new suit—the expected uniform for all of Xecutive's drivers.

Cabbing was one of the few jobs that a black man could still get in London without too much aggro. Campbell was so tired of being broke that he was up for hearing any suggestion about ways to make a little money and when Trevor suggested the driving, he was sceptical at first. He didn't want it to sound like a snub, but he couldn't see himself as a cab driver, luxury cars or not. He could sell, that was his strong point. He could sell shoes, make-up, vacuum cleaners, whatever…he could even sell cars, but drive cars for a living…?

Trevor reasoned that Campbell was desperate and as sales jobs weren't so easy to come by anymore, he had to take what he could get.

Campbell had thought about it long and hard before deciding. The thing that convinced him was the use of a luxury car. With the Jag thrown in, the job didn't seem so bad. The pay was still crap, but just bearable.

The one thing that keeps you going when you grow up with nothing in a world where money equals freedom is the knowledge that it's not always going to be like that. Everything was just for a time and your time would surely come. You would make sure it came, just as soon as you were old enough. You were going to work twice as hard as your parents—twenty-four seven if necessary, to make sure you weren't at the bottom end for the rest of your life. Whenever things wore him down and he tired of the struggle, childhood memories flashed through Campbell's mind. Memories of a father who was unable to take care of himself let alone his son after his wife died. A man who soaked himself in drink while his son was forced to learn to feed himself or starve in a house which had long been condemned as unfit for human habitation.

Campbell was a positive thinker, though, and none of that made him resentful. If anything it made him stronger, for he knew how easy it was to slip back into poverty and the childhood memories were stark reminders that poverty was a place he didn't want to revisit.

Most of the people were already seated at the forty or so dining tables spread out in the elegant ballroom on the hotel's grand floor. A stunning dark-skinned woman in a sequinned black silk dress took their tickets at the door and with an inviting smile welcomed them in, then showed them to their table.

Trevor looked around him, impressed. There were women wherever you looked. Beautiful black women of every shape, shade and size. Women who had dressed like they were princesses and who displayed their latest hair creation proudly. Ladies with style and grace. Some there to make business contacts, some there to make social contacts, some there simply for a night out with their friends, but some there to meet Mr Right, a man with as much style and grace as they had and who could match them when it came to finance and career.

The few men there were outnumbered two to one.

"Check out the honeys in the place to be!" Trevor said to Campbell as they sat down on their table. "We should be doing this every week, man. You see what you've been missing with all that nonsense talk of yours."

At their table were five women and one other man. Delroy, as he introduced himself, was a financial consultant. Trevor told him that that was a pity as his finances didn't need consulting at the moment.

"Yes, I work for some of the big names," Delroy was telling Grace, the woman beside him. "Strictly blue chip companies. When it comes to investments, I'm the man." Delroy handed her his business card proudly and then pulled out a fat cigar from his pocket and lit it.

Grace grimaced and waved the fumes back in his face. "Do you mind?"

Trevor had already launched himself into a conversation with the woman to the other side of him. "So what's your name?" he was asking.

Sheree was her name and dressed in a dark red sequinned dress, it looked like sherry was her flavour.

"So what's your number?" he asked next, handing her a business card.

Campbell smiled. Good old Trevor, when it came to women, he didn't have time for the niceties like, "What are your interests? Are you with someone or did you come alone?" But even with the same old "What's your name, what's your size, what's your number?" he still managed to get a smile out of Sheree. It was the way he said it.

The five-course meal was delicious, well worth every penny of the steep entrance fee. And there were also a couple of chilled bottles of champagne on each table. Campbell was enjoying himself and soon engaged in a conversation with Claudette, the women next to him, who told him she was a barrister.

"Haven't I seen you in court before?" she asked him.

Campbell assured her that she hadn't and that he stayed away from places like that.

"Not even jury service?"

"They'll have to catch me first."

"So what do you do for a living?" Claudette asked.

"I run my own business," he said. Trevor had told him to say that. Told him that he didn't want Campbell shaming him up in front of nice and decent people. Anyway, it was true in a way.

"Doesn't everybody?" she asked mysteriously. "What kind of business exactly."

Campbell coughed. "I buy and sell cars."

The dinner done, a cabaret act and a comedian warmed up the guests until the energy picked up and people were about ready for the main event—the music. The sound system blasted loud and clear and from the first tune the majority of the guests were up on the dancefloor, with or without a partner, shaking their thing with wild abandon. That's the way James Brown makes you feel when he shouts, *"Get uppa, get on up, stay on the scene, get on up, like a sex machine, get on up. Get uppa..."*

James more or less brought down the house with that one. But there was more to come. The dancefloor was throbbing and overflowing with eager ravers.

Campbell danced a couple of numbers with Claudette, who seemed to have taken a fancy to him. He liked her and all that, but he was determined to make sure she understood that he had learned to say 'no'. He just didn't know how to tell her. She seemed to have already decided that he was her target for tonight and if her looks didn't capture him, she intended to talk him into a corner. Fortunately, she had to go to the ladies' room and Campbell took the opportunity to dip off the dancefloor and go to the very back of the ballroom, where he could stand in the shadows, sipping a cool glass of champagne and checking out the vibes on his own. He didn't want any loose women around him thinking that he was going to end up sleeping with one of them tonight. Because that was certainly Trevor's intention, whether he denied it or not. This was another set-up to get him hooked up with a babe. Trevor was determined that his spar should get his rocks off tonight. Campbell had to admit that, from what he could see, there were some real honeys in

23

the place. He could even see some ladies who he would consider to have his baby.

"You going to be here for a while?"

Campbell spun round, it was Claudette. She had found him. She had a smile on her face.

Campbell nodded.

"Well can you watch my things?" she said, thrusting her handbag upon him. "I'm just going to whine up my waist a little," she grinned.

Campbell watched her pert bottom as she disappeared onto the dancefloor. He sucked in some air. He felt awkward with the handbag, it was cramping his style. He slung it over the back of a chair. She said watch it, he could watch it from there.

It was then that he noticed her, sitting on a table not far away. An African princess, the jewel in the crown of beauties in attendance and she was smiling, *yes*, she was smiling at him. And that smile seemed to melt away any resistance he may have had and made his legs feel like jelly.

She was dressed like royalty in a patterned wrapper and blouse of African materials which looked like they had been designed by Yves St Laurent. She carried herself impressively and had some magical eyes which seemed to twinkle and tease in the semi-darkness of the ballroom. He watched her. A man sat beside her, talking animatedly. She listened politely, but Campbell could tell from her eyes that the escort was failing to light her fire. Wasn't that a yawn she stifled when she put her fingers to her lips? Campbell sighed. This was a woman he had to meet. If only he were there by her side now, she would inspire him to speak in verses.

He remained in the shadows, thinking and waiting for an opportunity. Hoping beyond hope that the man would leave her unattended, so that he could rope in and exchange a word or two with her. With his eyes he undressed her. *No not that!* his mind was screaming, *you've learned to say 'no'!* But he couldn't, he couldn't...he couldn't decline to sleep with her if he got the opportunity. She was the bomb!

"Oh, I must be getting old, I've only danced a couple of numbers and I'm out of breath already." It was Claudette. Campbell looked up and smiled, but his mind was elsewhere. "I think I'll just sit down here for a minute," she said, flopping down on the same chair her handbag hung from. "Aren't you going to dance some more?"

Campbell shook his head. "I'm alright at the moment, you know."

"What's the matter, don't you like the music?"

No, he said, it wasn't that. He was just chilling out a bit.

"I know what you mean, it's hot on the dancefloor."

Campbell's heart fluttered as the African Princess again looked over in his direction. He greeted her eyes with what he thought was an alluring smile and he saw what he thought was a glow on her face. At the same time, Claudette poked him in his stomach to get his attention.

"Are you going deaf?" she asked.

"What?"

"I was saying that I'm tired of going to parties with more women than men. It's typical. Where are all the black men? Why don't they come out and support their own functions?"

Campbell shrugged. How the hell would he know? "I'm here aren't I?"

"Yes, but you're probably here because you knew that it was going to be more women than men so you would have more women to choose from," she said, scanning the room for any stray male who may have entered.

Campbell assured her that that wasn't the case. That definitely wasn't the case. For one thing, he was only interested in one woman in the venue. That was what he was thinking but he didn't say. He looked up to where the

25

Princess was sitting. *Damn!* She was gone. *Damn!* He scoured the ballroom to see if he could see her. He recognised her African costume out on the dancefloor.

"Yes! This is one of my favourite tunes!" Claudette cried out as the deejay dropped the Sounds of Blackness' *The Pressure*, to the general approval of the guests. "Watch my bag!" she called out as she went off on the dancefloor again.

Campbell shifted position slightly to get a better view of the Princess who was now throwing down as well as anybody out there. Her escort was still there, dancing opposite her. It seemed like he was stuck to her like glue as he had been all evening. It didn't look like he was going to give another man a squeeze to get anywhere near her. Campbell could see that that wasn't where she was at…she needed more than this guy. If he was going to make it, he would have made it by now.

Campbell kept watching, one number after the other, planning in his head how he was going to do this. He just wanted to tell her how beautiful she looked which would possibly get a smile out of her. After that, he might just…who knows?

She danced for another half an hour, before returning to her table, still accompanied by Mister Superglue. This time, Campbell wasn't playing. He was going to go up to her.

He walked over slowly, still unsure of exactly what he was going to say, he just wanted to let her know the inexplicable way she was making him feel and he would tell from the way she responded whether or not he stood a chance. The look in the eyes was always a dead giveaway. As for Mister Stick-By-You, he wasn't too worried about cutting in on him. For one thing, he looked like a pussy and for another thing getting a chance to chat to this woman was worth any amount of distress from the man she was with. Besides, maybe she wasn't *with* him.

They didn't notice him when he got there. He stood

awkwardly for a moment while the man—tall with relaxed hair—attempted to impress the African Princess with a raucous story about how his horse bolted from him while he was out riding. Campbell coughed loudly, trying to butt into the conversation.

"Excuse me," he said, trying to catch the attention of the African Princess.

The man with the wet-look hair broke off his story to look up. "Oh waiter, another bottle of champagne for this table please." He continued with his story.

Campbell simply stood there, glaring at the man. This wasn't the time or place, but, where he came from, a man could get a slap for that mistake.

"I'm not the waiter," he said loud enough for everybody on the table to hear.

His story interrupted again, the man looked up. "In that case…with all due respect, can you buzz off? As I was saying Dionne…"

If it wasn't for the fact that they were in an upmarket hotel at a prestigious event with some quality people, Wet-look might have received two slaps. As it was, in the heat of the moment, he was tongue-tied and speechless. The man had killed any attempt on Campbell's part to say what he had to say and all he could do was walk back to his position with his confidence crushed. But he wasn't going to forget this.

Being the old-fashioned type of guy he was, Campbell held the front passenger door of the Jaguar open for Claudette and stole a glance at her well-shaped backside, before climbing in on the driver's side. Claudette was a woman who oozed sex in the way she walked and the way she talked.

"So where are we going?" he asked her.

"Anywhere you'd like. It's up to you," she said in her husky voice while taking an impressive look around the immaculate interior of the car. "I'll tell you what, let's forget the late night movie and just go to my place and check out my jacuzzi," she said, with a naughty look in her eyes.

"Where do you live?"

"On the other hand, you don't have to drive me home just yet…the night is still young and I know of a really nice bar in Soho we could go to for a drink."

"If I have any more to drink I won't be able to drive you home at all. Maybe we could go out for a drink another time."

"Well, if you're sure," Claudette said with a hint of disappointment. "I live in Wandsworth."

Campbell switched on the ignition and immediately, the sound of Barry White filled the car. Easing the car gently away from the kerbside, he headed south.

"It's such a beautiful night," Claudette remarked, leaning back comfortably against the headrest. "This night was made for loving."

Campbell had to agree there was something magical in the air.

"What business did you say you own again?"

Campbell winced. He had forgotten he'd said that in a moment of low-esteem when everyone else at the ball was announcing loudly what they did for a living. He wished he hadn't lied. But it was too late. He now felt too ashamed to admit that he was a chauffeur and before he knew it he was spinning the untruth again.

"I'm in the car business."

"Oh that's right…well, you must be doing very well for yourself because this is a really nice car."

"So what do you do for a living again?" he asked.

She reminded him that she was a barrister and probably one of the most successful black barristers in Britain. She was successful, she said, because she worked hard. So hard in fact that she never normally had time to go out to evenings like tonight.

"I'm too busy for that. That's why I'm still single. All my friends and family keep asking me when I'm going to get married, as if a girl hasn't got anything more important than marriage to think about. I tell them straight that I've got a lot of living to do first, but I'm sure they think it's because I can't find a man. Nothing could be further from the truth. Getting a man isn't a problem, I can get a man any day of the week. What's more difficult is getting rid of a man who's not right. That's not to say, of course, that if the right guy came along that I wouldn't think about it. But I want a real man for a change. There are so many imposters out there. I want a man, not an excuse for a man, a man who understands that I'm a real woman and who understands all my needs as a real woman. When I find that man I'm prepared to give him anything he wants as long as he takes care of me and gives me what I need."

Claudette had a lot to say and liked to talk. Campbell was a good listener when he wanted to be and this was one of those times. It took another half an hour through the midnight traffic to reach her flat in Wandsworth. During that time he had learned that Claudette was the niece of the Prime Minister of Guyana and the daughter of an eminent doctor and of a mother who was herself a leading lawyer back home. She had two brothers, one was a fireman and the other a karate instructor.

But all that mattered little to Campbell. It felt like she was reading him her CV to impress. She didn't need to. He was impressed anyway.

"I hope I'm not boring you. As you can gather I love to talk. That's why I like criminal law so much. I enjoy speaking in front of a jury. I'm good at it, one of the best. It's a profession dominated by men and sometimes a girl has to use everything in her power to get her way. You see, to be a good barrister you've got to be prepared to do almost anything to win your case. I've got this recurring fantasy of stripping off in front of a male jury as I'm doing my summing up, just to make sure they decide in favour of my client. Do you have fantasies?"

Campbell said that he didn't, not any more.

"I don't even dream any more," he admitted. "I don't know what it is. I used to dream a lot. I used to have some really beautiful dreams. But I don't seem to any more."

"Of course you have dreams, everybody does. It's just that you don't remember them. The thing to do is to try and remember your dreams as soon as you wake up every morning. I dream every night. And I've been having some particularly raunchy dreams lately."

Campbell took the Vauxhall Bridge route and was soon heading towards Battersea.

"So this business of yours, how much do you earn?"

Campbell told her in a friendly way that it was none of her business. He was feeling really bad about the lie, but what could he do?

"Well, I don't mind telling you how much I earn…it's no big secret. I'm on £80,000 a year."

Campbell almost choked. "£80,000!"

"It's not all that much," she said, "when you consider that I'm self-employed and there are lots of hidden costs like the cost of chambers and my clerk and so on."

It was like Campbell didn't hear any of that. £80,000 was £80,000 to him. Claudette had gone up in his estimation.

"But you must be earning something around that?"

"Something around that," he heard himself mutter unconvincingly.

With her salary in mind, Campbell expected her home to be lavish, but Claudette lived in a surprisingly modest flat overlooking the river in a former council block turned yuppie building which was protected by high-security electric gates and a TV intercom at the entrance. It was after 2am when they arrived and despite the long journey home, Campbell was reluctant to take up Claudette's offer to go in for a cup of coffee.

"Are you sure you won't?"

Campbell thought about it some more.

"I live here alone, you know," she said with a sweet smile.

It was tempting, but…

There was an awkward stalemate. Claudette broke the silence first by changing the subject entirely.

"You know, Jags are my favourite car. I've always wanted one myself. Isn't the petrol really expensive in these?"

"Sure, bloody. I cause an energy crisis every time I fill her up."

"So why do you drive such a gas guzzler, or is it a 'pulling machine'."

"You think I've got time to drive around trying to get laid? Please."

"But isn't this just an extension of your penis?"

Campbell gave her a look that said he didn't find that funny. She told him to lighten up, it was only a joke.

"I'm a comedian, my mouth is always getting me in trouble. But seriously, you must have had women come onto you just because you've got a nice car."

"No, not all the time. It takes more than a nice car to impress women these days, because you've even got ragamuffins driving around in Jags now."

"Damn right. Forget about the extension, just give me a penis. That's what I say."

She laughed. Campbell grinned.

"What about you? You must have a lot of guys interested in you because you've got a successful career."

31

"Yes, I've got to admit that being a barrister does seem to turn men on. It's as if I'm the first woman they've met who has got any real power."

They sat in the car for almost an hour, outside her block. Most of the time engaged in pleasant chit chat, sometimes straying on the verge of intimacy but all very properly. It started off with pretty innocent stuff.

She told him about the church she belonged to and he asked her if it was true that there's ten women to every man in the church nowadays. She was particularly interested in knowing about his last girlfriend and why he didn't have a woman now —"Are you sure you don't?" *Like I don't know!* Then she asked him what music he preferred to make love to. He told her Marvin Gaye, Al Green or maybe D'Angelo. "That Brown Sugar—damn!" She said that classical music was the sex music of her choice. Campbell grinned, he could have guessed. Claudette had made it clear all evening that she was anything but the typical black woman, letting him know that he should count himself fortunate that she deemed him worthy of sharing her companionship.

Before he knew it, Campbell was drifting off. He was thinking of driving off into the sunset in a little red convertible, the wind rushing through his hair and with his African Princess beside him. He thought of how he would kiss her all over, love her all over and give her everything she needed. He even thought about his oath of celibacy, but his heart was telling him to follow her star and it was too easy not to ask why. It was even easier to simply hitch his heart onto the ride to see if it would take him to the land of happiness at the end of his rainbow.

Claudette was still talking. Campbell tried to stifle a yawn but was unsuccessful and had to apologise.

"No carry on," he insisted, "I enjoy talking to you."

"Look, I can see you're too tired. Are you sure you don't want to stay the night? There's lots of room. I won't be able to relax if I think of you driving all that way back to north London at this time of night and falling asleep on the way. It is dangerous, you know."

Campbell had to admit that he wasn't looking forward to the drive back either. He really could use some rest.

"Well then come in," she said invitingly.

Claudette's one bedroom flat was extremely tidy and well furnished with a woman's touch. She gave Campbell a quick tour: the large kitchen/diner, the compact living room with the wide screen television in the corner and the bookcase full of oversized leather bound books and the bedroom which, Campbell couldn't help noticing, had an ambience of sensual splendour with satin sheets, a king-size bed, candlelight and soft music the moment you hit the light switch.

"As you're staying, we might as well have a real drink. Coffee will only keep you awake all night. And we don't want that now, do we?" Claudette suggested, pouring out a couple of brandies.

Campbell sipped at the brandy, all the time aware that he needed to hold back just in case. It would be too easy to allow the combination of an alluring woman and sexual frustration to get in the way of his determination to say 'no'. He had to maintain his self-control, even if it meant putting physical distance between Claudette and himself.

"I don't have many women friends," Claudette said. "I relate to men much better. You see, I understand everything about men. I know exactly what you want. I know you don't want a relationship. And that's fine by me. You see Campbell, like you I get bored easily. So when it comes to sex, I want variety. I want one man on Monday and another on Tuesday. A different man for every day of the week."

"Do you never get lonely living here by yourself?"

"Only when I'm awakened on a Sunday morning by neighbours bonking their heads off. We're all vulnerable in bed. What I need is to have a man with me to hold me tight. What are you doing on Saturday night? Wouldn't you like to wake up with me on Sunday morning?"

Campbell grinned.

"Sure. Sure I'd like to. That's my problem, I can never say 'no'. But I'm learning."

Claudette found this very amusing and laughed heartily.

"That's what they all say. What I find is that when a man says 'no', he really means 'yes'. Some say 'yes' immediately and others take their time, but they all say 'yes' in the end."

Just to prove her point, she guessed correctly that he had a weak spot and the next thing he knew a dainty hand had dived down into the front of his trousers taking hold of his weakness and with a click of Claudette's fingers he was hard for her sweetness. With a look of victory on her face she said, "I told you so…" She was in control and that was another reason he didn't want to sleep with her, but with her hand wrapped around his point of least resistance, the reasons not to were fading from his consciousness.

"You must spend an awful lot of time masturbating," she purred in his ear.

Campbell insisted that he didn't. That he didn't do that sort of thing, but from the smirk on her face, Claudette didn't believe him one bit. "You should be relaxed about it. Everybody does it." She gave his crotch another gentle squeeze. "I know you're horny for me," she gushed. "I'm going to make it good for you tonight, soooooooo good. I'm going to give you something to think about, all night long. I'm soooooooooo ready."

Campbell couldn't deny that he was horny. The bulge in his trousers was there for all to see. All this erotic talk had exploded his willpower. There was something about her upfront attitude that made him believe that he was going to enjoy making love to her. Claudette continued working his balls expertly like a gambler fondles a pair of dice before rolling them. She said that she had chosen him of all the men at the Ebony Club, because she wanted him to make love to her in every way possible.

She whispered a couple of suggestions in his ear, which both amazed and turned him on. Then before he knew what was going on, she lifted up her top to reveal the black lace bra which held her small breasts.

Claudette was a woman who had an erotic imagination, but a pornographic inclination. She excused herself to fetch some things from the bedroom and returned a short while later with a duffel bag stuffed with an assortment of adult toys and a set of raunchy undies designed to attract a man and keep him. Campbell looked on with a hint of trepidation as one by one Claudette pulled out an assortment of vibrators and stimulators, a whip, a pair of handcuffs and a huge dildo.

Campbell said that he didn't think that he was into anything like that at all.

"You've never tried vibrators?" she asked.

"Of course not...some of us can take care of business without that."

"Is that what you think? Well it's a good job you came home with me, because tonight you've got yourself your very own sex teacher. Tonight, I'm going to introduce you to the buried treasures—the most exquisite and forbidden joys of sex."

"Are you serious about the handcuffs?"

"They're optional...does it surprise you that I'm this sexual?"

Yes it did, Campbell had to admit. She seemed so conventional earlier. When she revealed that she was a barrister, he imagined she must be pretty straight. A straight missionary position woman if anything, but little did he know that under her cool, calm, and intellectually aloof exterior, she possessed a whole arsenal of tools.

After a couple more brandies, Campbell was anybody's. For no apparent reason, he leaned across to Claudette on the other side of the sofa and planted a wet, sloppy kiss on her forehead. She looked up to him and smiled. That was a signal for him to plant another kiss, this time on her lips and before he knew it they were gripped together in a tight embrace. His hot tongue darting into her mouth, Claudette gripping him hard by the buttocks and panting heavily.

"It's yours," she told him softly, "it's all yours…if you want it just take it, all of it."

From the sofa, they rolled onto the floor. Claudette knew exactly what she wanted and didn't need any tuition on giving him what he required either. She unbuttoned his shirt swiftly and sat astride him, working her tongue on every inch of his well-toned chest. Campbell took a good hard look at the patch of black hair on her crotch and caressed it gently like a long lost friend. A smile spread across his face.

Claudette liked to be in control. With one hand, she eased Campbell gently into her and with the other took his hand and urged him to caress her breasts. "No, not gently, not softly." She wanted him to knead them. "Yes, yesssssss…just like that."

As she rode atop him, she told him to take her firmly by the buttocks. Lying on his back, Campbell had no choice but to do as he was told. He closed his eyes to rely almost entirely on his sense of touch and found himself slipping slowly into ecstasy as Claudette's rhythm became more and more frenetic. He liked it. One moment she was going so fast that he might as well not have been there and the next she was going so slow he begged her to go faster. But she simply replied, "We'll do it my way."

He liked her. But there was one thing he didn't like about making love to her, and that was the fact that he couldn't get his mind off the African Princess, the woman he knew only by the name Dionne.

Suddenly, without warning, Claudette let out a high-pitched moan, loud enough to waken the whole neighbourhood as she shuddered in spasms for what seemed like an eternity. Then she collapsed on top of him, . exhausted.

Campbell listened as her breathing calmed and his mind began to wander. He started thinking of the woman he would rather have got off with. Why hadn't he said anything to her? Why had he been so paralysed? Maybe Trevor was right, maybe he was losing his touch. Why had he taken Claudette home when he really wanted to be with African Princess?

"Okay, it's your turn," Claudette said, rolling over on her back.

Yes, it was his turn, but Campbell didn't feel like it. Even if he had, he was unable to because he had gone limp. But that didn't deter Claudette who went on her knees to apply her hot tongue to his balls—expertly, as she juggled them carefully in her hands. But all to no avail. Campbell didn't even have the minimum stiffness in him. Oh well, there was only one thing for it, Claudette decided, rolling over to her side and pulling out the huge black dildo from the duffel bag.

The night's unexpected adventure had worn him out. Claudette had been an experience and he knew that if he so desired he could have many exciting sexual adventures with her. But that was it. It wouldn't go any further than that.

The next morning Claudette was up first and already dressed while Campbell resisted the urgency to drag himself out of what seemed like the deepest and most irresistible sleep. He had never felt better. In his dreamland, he and Dionne had waltzed under a waterfall of rose petals and she had sung him a love song with the sweetest melody. And together they had floated on a raft of romance, down the unpredictable river of life, with the sun above shining bright wherever they went.

"You're going to have to leave," she said, "because I'm going to work."

Campbell was still floating down that river and suggested that she could go on without him and that he would let himself out afterwards.

"I don't do that," Claudette said. "Just because we've slept together, it doesn't mean I trust you enough to leave you alone in my home…"

From the tone of her voice it was no use arguing. Campbell was going to have to dip at the same time.

He dragged himself up and after a quick shower was ready to leave also.

"Off to your business?" she asked as he climbed in the car.

The question reminded Campbell of the lie he had told the night before. He felt uncomfortable about maintaining the deception and and decided to come clean.

"Look, I exaggerated a bit. I don't have any successful business. I make a living driving people around in the Jag."

"You're a chauffeur?"

"Something like that."

Claudette laughed so loudly it looked undignified.

"A chauffeur! I almost guessed right. You see, I always try to figure out what a man really does when I meet him. Whatever he says he does I always take into consideration that he's trying to impress me, so I make allowances for a reduction. I thought you were a truck driver. It wasn't far off was it?"

72% of black men say they fantasize about someone they haven't slept with and find their thoughts turning to sex when they're at work. Men who have only had one partner almost never fantasize at work, whereas those who have had ten or more partners have a strong tendency to let their thoughts wander to sex whilst in the office.

THREE'S A CROWD

The Jaguar eased past Camden Town tube station, heading towards Chalk Farm. Behind the wheel, Campbell could barely resist the temptation to pump up the gas some. He finally got a chance to accelerate as the car breezed up Haverstock Hill, through Belsize Park, past the trendy cafes and restaurants with French names. Not a black face in sight. He eased up at the sight of the familiar blue light of a police station up ahead, the thought crossing his mind that the combination of a black man and a criss motor was enough on its own to get him pulled in this neighbourhood without having to distress the situation some more with some nifty driving. *A' so it go sometime.*

With one hand on the steering wheel, he took the notepad off the dash and checked the address once more. He knew the road, it was a couple more blocks up on the right.

Number 33 was an impressive two-storey white villa, set back from the road in landscaped gardens which literally backed onto the Heath, with a new registration Mercedes convertible parked in its gravel driveway. A whistle escaped Campbell's lips as he took in an eyeful of the splendour before him. He had seen some nice properties since working for Xecutive, but this had to be the best. He parked in front of the gates and climbed out, nodding his head approvingly at everything he saw. This was the kind of house he would get himself one day. This is the kinda house! He opened the gate and walked slowly up the gravel path to the front door. He rang the doorbell and waited. "Just a minute!" came a woman's voice from within.

Campbell stepped back and waited by the car, his gaze still fixed on the house, trying to figure out how much it cost. A place like this definitely didn't come cheap. There was even a tennis court to one side.

A moment later, a well dressed woman stepped out of the front door of the villa, looking very business-like and carrying an attache case. Campbell's jaw dropped. He hadn't expected a black woman.

In the two weeks he had worked at Xecutive Cars, he had only chauffeured one black person—a West African diplomat. The type of people who tended to use the company were well enough off to be able to afford the extra cost of a cab company with luxury cars. If you booked a cab from Xecutive, a new model Jaguar or Mercedes arrived and you were driven in style. As well as individual clients, the company was regularly used for corporate entertainment and was the preferred limousine service for several of the major TV companies to transport celebrity guests to and from their studios.

Campbell held the back door open, a big grin on his face. The woman smiled politely at him as she stepped gracefully into the rear. Campbell closed the door gently after her and made his way around the back of the car to the driver's side and climbed in. Still grinning, he glanced at the notepad, then looked at the lady in his rearview mirror:

"To Parliament Square?"

"Yes, that's right," she answered with the sweetest smile.

Campbell could hardly contain himself. This woman had real class. She looked like she was accustomed to flying first class, if not by private jet; like she was a lady used to mink coats and diamond necklaces and who drank nothing but champagne and ate only at the finest restaurants.

Everything about her had a mark of wealth about it—the way she talked, the way she walked, her poise and aura and the expensive perfume which wafted gently behind her. He stole another glance in the mirror as he pulled away from the kerbside and executed a U-turn. Her looks and youthful air made her seem like she was in her early forties but Campbell guessed that she was probably older but had succeeded in keeping her figure into middle age. She wore her hair straight and styled very conservatively. Her skin looked fresh, with just the subtlest hint of make-up and her lipstick shone a succulent deep red as she scanned through the pink pages of the Financial Times.

"Excuse me," Campbell asked politely, as he turned back down the Hill, heading towards the city, "I hope you don't mind me asking...but that house back there, you own it?"

The woman looked up from her paper and nodded.

"Yes...why?"

"No reason," Campbell beamed, but couldn't resist adding, "Nice...nice."

The woman leaned back in the seat and continued her scanning. Campbell couldn't resist interrupting her again.

"I'd just like to say 'nuff respect. It's good to see some of our people living large, you know. Look, I hope I'm not interrupting your reading..."

The woman looked up from her paper. As obvious as it was that that was exactly what Campbell was doing, she smiled sweetly as if nothing could have been further from the truth.

Reassured, Campbell continued. "I hope you don't mind me asking...what do you do for a living?"

"I'm a member of Parliament."

"Member of Parliament!" Campbell turned his head briefly in acknowledgement. "Well...really, I've got to say another 'nuff respect. Member of Parliament...that is...that's brilliant. He glanced at her in the rearview mirror.

He recognised her now. "Wait a minute...you're that Tory MP aren't you...erm...Valerie Owen."

The woman nodded. Of course, Campbell was thinking, of course, that was who she was. Even with his scanty knowledge of British politricks, as he liked to call it, he knew who Valerie Owen was. The whole country now knew who Valerie Owen was since her victory in a by-election had led her to become Britain's first Afro-Caribbean Tory MP. And he, like nearly everybody in the black community— Tory or not—had a certain sense of pride when she declared in her victory speech that she was a "black woman first and Tory MP second". He warmed to the steady sexual glow telegraphed by her smile and her teasing, laughing eyes. Boy, she looked even more attractive in the flesh than she did on TV.

"Well congratulations on winning the by-election. Even though I don't vote myself, and even when I used to vote, I never voted Tory, nevertheless I would have voted for you if I was living in...where was it? Brent, wasn't it?"

Valerie Owen MP nodded.

"So why don't you vote?"

"Well...that's a good question. I used to, you know. Used to vote Labour, like everybody else I know. Voted for Diane Abbott when I was living over Hackney way. But that was a waste of time. The main reason black people vote is so that we can get someone in there to represent. You know what I'm saying? I mean, Bernie Grant's okay, but that other one...whassisname? Paul Boateng? He needs to go *black* home!"

Valerie smiled, throwing her head back gracefully. "I couldn't agree with you more."

"If you don't mind, Mrs O, you can do just one thing for me when you're up there in that House of Commons: please fight for all these youths who ain't got jobs. Every day I hear people saying black youths doing this and black youths doing that and it's coming like every little thing that happens the youths get the blame. But I know a lot of youths, you know, pure talented youth, and they ain't got nothing to do. And they ain't getting the chances either."

"Rest assured, I take every opportunity to remind the Secretary of State of just that."

Campbell smiled. "I was sure you would anyway...I was just reminding you."

Going back through Camden Town, he took the one-way system and sped through Mornington Crescent. He didn't hit trouble until he got halfway down Gower Street where the afternoon traffic had ground to a noisy, fuming halt.

"By the way my name is Campbell...Campbell Clarke," he said turning and stretching out his hand. She shook it.

"Nice to meet you Campbell."

"Here's my number," he said, handing her one of the newly printed business cards on the dash. "If you need a driver...at any time of the day or night, no problem...just give me a call."

"A personal service," she said with a pearl-toothed smile.

"That's right," Campbell said. He had been thinking of doing this anyway. Screw Louie. Why should that fat git be getting ninety percent of everything he earned? All Louie had to do was own a phone and lease a few cars and that entitled him to almost everything the drivers made. That couldn't be right. The reason he had bought the mobile phone and got the business cards printed in the first place was so that he could get a little private business of his own going. "Just call me up, wherever you are," he continued. "You might be trying to get home from an event or something, just give me a call, tell me where you are and I'll come and pick you up."

"Yes, I'll remember that," she said, tucking the business card into her attache case. "I'm all for recycling the black pound," she said with a subtle wink. "You must spend a lot of your time in traffic like this…"

"You can say that again," Campbell sighed. "Definitely. Driving isn't the job for me. It's just a nice little earner. What I really want to do is set up my own business."

"Really? That's interesting. What type of business?"

"Oh…I haven't decided yet. Maybe property. How come you MPs are always complaining about not earning enough money? It looks to me like you're doing alright for yourself." Campbell grinned. "Your house must have cost a bob or two."

"Oh, politics didn't pay for my house. On the contrary, it will probably cause me to lose it," she laughed.

"How can you afford to live there then…? If it's none of my business, then just say so."

"You seem so well up on your politics, I thought you would know anyway…the clue is in my surname."

"Owen?"

"Yes, as in Owen Foods. You might have used my Owen's Hot Caribbean Sauces in your food."

"Is that you as well?!" Campbell was even more impressed. "I never knew…"

What could he say? He was filled with a real sense of pride. It was refreshing to meet a black person who had real power in the world. Not a pop singer or an athlete, but a politician. Valerie Owen was inspirational because she had something solid to show for all her labours and Campbell began to feel an urgency in his mind to also do something constructive with his life. He had to stop thinking about starting a business and really get something together. The more he talked to Mrs Owen, the more he wanted to be like her. Successful.

"So, what would you say is the secret of your success?"

"There's no secret to success," she answered. "You've just got to be prepared whenever opportunities arise. I work

45

hard at what I do and I've been blessed with an ability which I don't take lightly. I try to use the little talent I have in the best positive way and just try and get better in what I do."

"Looking at me now, do you think I'll become successful?"

"I don't see why not, if you keep those stars in your eyes and your dreams between your teeth. And if you remember, there's two ways to die: young and old and dying young is the worst possible way. You'll go far in this world, if you try hard not to die young."

With those supportive words, Campbell continued driving down Shaftesbury Avenue. He swung a left at Charing Cross Road, and from there the rest of the route was clear. He pulled up at Parliament Square in front of the entrance to the Commons. Holding the rear door open for her, he reminded her that she should feel free to call if she ever needed. She looked in his eyes briefly and smiled. "If I need anything, I'll call," she promised. "I could use a reliable driver."

In that moment, a thought crossed Campbell's mind. An impossible thought. Apart from anything else, she belonged to a world that he could only dream about. Women like that don't even notice guys like him. Then there was the age thing, and besides, he had learned to say 'no'.

13% of black men rate their sexual performance as 'average'. 24% think it's 'a little better than most' and 53% believe it's a lot better. 2% rate themselves as a little worse than most. 8% say they don't know. Nobody said they were a lot worse.

FOUR PLAY

The time was just after eight when Campbell pulled up outside Trevor's place, looking forward to hitting the sack for an early night. He had only just arrived when the mobile rang.

"Hello…Campbell Clarke? It's Valerie Owen. How close are you to the House of Commons? Could you pick me up in twenty minutes? I'll be standing by the main entrance. Yes. I'm going home to Hampstead. Okay, I'll see you then."

As exhausted as he was, somehow Campbell managed to bring himself to turn the ignition on again, execute a perfect U-turn and with a roar of tyres head back into the city.

Just hearing Mrs Owen's voice had rekindled a spark in him. This was one customer he wanted to know well and he was already trying to figure out ways in which she could be of help to him. No way did he want to mess things up with her. She wanted a car in twenty minutes and he was going to be there in twenty minutes.

Campbell had been driving Valerie Owen on an irregular basis for two weeks now and had managed to combine his private work for her with his work for Xecutive Cars without too much problem. The lives of MPs being what they are, she needed a car when business was slack. Campbell made every effort to accommodate her and in those two weeks he had learned a little about her.

Punctuality was one of Valerie Owen's traits. When she said she was going to be somewhere at a certain time, that's exactly what she meant and she expected the same punctuality from her associates. Fortunately for Campbell, he arrived just in time and she didn't have to stand on Parliament Square for more than a few seconds.

"So how are you doing today, Mrs O?" he asked, holding the back door open for her."

"Very well Campbell, very well…just a bit exhausted. It's been one of those tiring days…in and out of the lobbies voting, you know."

"Anything interesting?" he asked, climbing in the driver's seat and pulling out to head north.

"Same old politics…sometimes I wonder if I'm not wasting my time there."

"You hang on in there Mrs O, we need more of your kind in parliament. Believe!"

"Don't worry, I'm not about to give up just yet. I'm just feeling disillusioned, that's all. It's a temporary thing."

"Put your feet up on the back seat if you want to Mrs O. Don't mind me. Wait a minute, I think I've got just the thing to relax you…"

With one hand on the steering wheel, he lifted up the cassette compartment between the front seats and flicked through the selection until he found what he wanted. He slipped the cassette into the stereo and turned up the volume slightly as the hoarse voice of Louis Armstrong singing *What A Wonderful World* filled the car.

"You like jazz?" Mrs Owen asked, a look of satisfaction spreading across her face.

"Yeah, some…not everything, you know. I'm really a soul man myself, with a little bit of reggae, a little club music."

"Oh, you should meet my daughter. She's always burning the candle at both ends to go to the clubs."

"Yeah? Then I'm looking forward to meeting her. I hope I get the chance. I'm sure we'll have a lot to talk about."

"I'm sure you will."

Valerie Owen had managed to combine bringing her daughter up singlehandedly with building a successful business. By all accounts she was a shrewd business woman who had built a flourishing empire from selling patties on a stall in Dalston Market just twenty years ago. She was also polite and generous and she and Campbell got on very well together. He had even made a tape of some old-time blue beat and mento for her, when she mentioned that she was still partial to the music of her Caribbean youth.

They eventually arrived at Mrs Owen's Hampstead home. Campbell remembered the Mercedes Benz parked in the driveway. Alongside it now was a baby blue Suzuki Vitara jeep with the word 'Playgirl' emblazoned on its rear.

"My daughter's home," Mrs Owen mumbled to herself. Campbell climbed out and went around the car to hold the door open for her.

"Any time, Mrs O," Campbell reminded her as she walked up her garden path. "You've got my hotline number, just call."

As he turned to climb in the Jag, he heard a woman's voice call out.

"Mom, is that a taxi?"

Campbell looked up to see a woman at the doorway of Mrs Owen's house, her jacket half on and half off. "Driver, hold on!" she called out to him and, rushing out, managed a quick hug and kiss for her mother, before jumping into the back seat of the Jaguar.

"Sweeeeeeeeet!" Campbell heard himself whistle, dragging out the word for all its sensuality. Whether she heard it or not, the exclamation was lost on her.

"I'm going to the Blue Note in Hoxton Square. But we're picking someone up on the way, in Primrose Hill," she told him officiously.

Campbell's first thought was to tell her that he wasn't for

hire. He was so tired now, he needed to get home, but when he turned around he recognised her. It was the woman from the Ebony Club, the woman he had been attracted to, the African Princess Dionne. His heart started beating fast, his feet were tingling.

"Sure thing," he said, with a smile on his face. So this was Mrs Owen's daughter? *Sweeeeet*.

Ignoring the no smoking sign behind the driver's seat, Dionne Owen pulled out a Silk Cut from a pack of twenty and lit it with her engraved zippo lighter, inhaled deeply and filled the car with a cloud of smoke. Campbell observed her in the rearview mirror. She wore a black leather waistcoat above a pair of bodyhugging yellow denim jeans and had her hair tucked into a floppy, woolly leopard-skin hat. Although she didn't look as glamorous as she did when he first saw her, she was every bit as attractive, every bit as alluring and full of pretty, feminine charm.

She obviously didn't recognise him.

"You're Mrs Owen's daughter," he said.

"You know Mum?"

"Sure. I'm her driver—personal driver, y'know. I'm Campbell by the way. Clarkey to my spars."

"Good for you." She blew out another puff of smoke.

As he drove back down Haverstock Hill, Campbell took the opportunity to strike up a conversation.

"Yes, your mum's always talking about you. You're a bit of a raver, aren't you?"

Dionne blew out another cloud of smoke, but didn't answer.

"What kind of music d'you like."

"All sorts."

"Yeah? For example?"

Dionne sighed as if she had better things to be doing in the back of a car. Then her mobile rang.

"…But Mike," she was saying, "I always celebrate my

birthday at home with my mother...she expects it from me...well that's very sweet of you, but we can go to the Savoy for dinner any day. My birthday only comes once a year...yes...yes...no it's not going to be a big deal, just my mother and a few close friends that's all...well look, it's up to you. If you want to celebrate my birthday with me tomorrow, then come by...if you don't that's alright. No, I'm not getting angry. It doesn't bother me, it really doesn't...yes...I'm in a cab...I'm going out...alright...that's fine, I'll see you when I see you."

With that she snapped shut the phone and kissed her teeth.

Campbell smiled sweetly at her reflection in the rearview mirror. "I like your hat..."

Dionne looked up. She blew out a cloud of smoke and nodded to him in acknowledgement.

"You know where I can get myself a hat like that?"

She waited until she had blown out another cloud of smoke before answering. "It was made for me actually," she said in a busy tone, "by a friend."

"Could you get your friend to make me one?"

She shrugged her shoulders. "If you can afford it...it wasn't cheap, you know."

Campbell shrugged off her tone. Okay, so she was a bit fiesty. That made her even more attractive to a man who had lost his mind to thoughts of love. She could trample all over him if she pleased and he would welcome it.

"Money's not a problem," he bragged. "Just ask your friend for me...here's my card."

With one hand on the steering wheel, he handed her a business card.

"Anytime you need a driver, just call that number. You never know, you might be coming out of a rave or something in the middle of the night and you can't get a cab, just give me a call. I'll come and pick you up, wherever you are. No problem."

Dionne nodded nonchalantly and continued smoking. Campbell studied her in the rearview mirror. He just needed a bit of time to get her in the mood for what he wanted to propose. He would save it, until they got to know each other a little better. As far as Campbell was concerned, he was definitely going to get to know this woman better. Especially now that he knew where she lived.

"That guy on the phone...sounded like a waste of time if you ask me."

Dionne looked as if she couldn't have agreed more, but she wasn't asking. She couldn't stop herself expressing her feelings however.

"I can't believe I was explaining everything to him...where I was, who I was with and everything...I should have told him where to go."

Even when she was angry, she was tantalising. Campbell was pleased to hear that she didn't have time for a guy who sounded like a complete asshole. He wondered if it was Mister Wet-look, hoped it was him, and wanted to tell Dionne that things didn't have to be like that, and that he knew a lot of really sensitive men who wouldn't behave like that. Men like himself who wanted to devote themselves to a woman like her and who would always show up on her birthday. From the look in her eye he could tell exactly what kind of loving she wanted. She wanted a man to whom she was prepared to give anything, as long as he took care of her and gave her what she needed. He wanted to tell her that he was that very man, but it was too soon. She wouldn't take him seriously.

"Honestly..." she said quietly to herself, "there's gotta be more to life than a man who can't make up his mind."

She took in a deep drag of her cigarette, puffed out slowly, then kissed her teeth.

"Was he your main squeeze or something?"

"Main nothing actually," she said, looking at Campbell properly for the first time. Why was she telling him all of this?

"Maaan, if you were my woman you would get anything you wanted." He stared at her hard in the rearview mirror, believing every word of it.

Dionne seemed not to have heard him, and stared blankly out of the car window, lost in her own thoughts.

Campbell was as sensitive as the next man and would have probably taken her attitude as a sign that she wasn't interested —if it was any other woman. Despite Dionne's lack of encouragement, he was determined to dig in for the winter if necessary and like any other player he felt that the longer he kept her talking the more chance he had. She had him spinning and he was enjoying it. It felt like his life was just about to begin.

He slipped on an Al Green cassette. Good old Al. When you got right down to it, he never let you down with his sultry vocals:

> *If I gave you my love*
> *I'll tell you what I'll do*
> *I expect a whole lot of love out of you*
> *You got to be good to me*
> *I'm gonna be good to you*
> *There's a whole lotta things you and I could do…*

"You like Al Green?"

Dionne nodded. "He's alright."

"My man knows how to sing a love song."

Dionne agreed.

"Of course, he's the Reverend Al Green now though, and that ain't the same thing. I heard that he's stopped singing all his horny tunes."

Dionne blew out the last few puffs from the cigarette. She

54

had a little smile on her face. She hit the button to wind down her window and threw the butt out.

"You know that smoking messes up your good looks, don't you?"

Dionne nodded unconcerned.

"Seriously. You look beautiful now, but you think about what your skin's going to look like in ten, fifteen years."

Dionne kissed her teeth, clearly unimpressed with Campbell's observation. She turned her head in a way that killed any further conversation, then hit the redial button on the mobile.

Damn! That was a really bad move, Campbell was thinking. *A really bad move.*

"Stella girl, we're outside your house now. Are you ready? Good. Okay see you in a moment."

She snapped the phone shut as cool as ice and told Campbell to stop the car in the middle of a terraced street of large and elegant Victorian houses. They sat there for a moment in silence, double parked, the engine ticking over. In another moment, the woman they were waiting for came out of her front door.

Dionne Owen and Stella De Souza could have passed for sisters. Not only did their rich chocolate complexions suggest a resemblance, but also, being best friends, they had similar taste and were prone to copycat dressing. Stella flopped into the back seat of the Jag, dressed in white denim jeans and a pale green leather waistcoat. On her head she wore a floppy woolly hat with a tigerskin pattern.

The two friends hugged and kissed each other on the cheeks as Campbell pulled away, heading for Shoreditch.

"So why are we going to this party? I thought you didn't like C. Riley," Dionne was saying.

"I didn't say that."

"Oh you're such a fibber, Stella. I remember your exact words when his video came up on the television—'here's

55

another black man with his brain in his dick'."

"I didn't say that did I?"

"You're kidding me…you kept on and on about how he had to stop calling women 'bitch' in his songs."

"Oh yes, I did didn't I? Well, he should. But it's hard to get really angry with him when you're too busy laughing at his lyrics. He's common, but funny as hell. I know, I should really despise him, but I got the invites and I just thought, why not? These record company parties are always such a giggle, there'll be lots of people we know there and…yes, I suppose I am a bit curious to see if he really is as smooth and sexy in the flesh as he is on record."

"That sounds like you want to get off with him," Dionne teased.

"Don't be silly, Dee Dee…that would be crazy. Good girls don't ask for it. You know how it is when somebody's voice does something for you on a CD…I'm just curious, that's all."

The traffic was going way too slow and Campbell's foot was itching. He wanted to drop the pedal and just go. He took the opportunity, as he eased the car through Kentish Town, to drop into the conversation.

"So you ladies are going to the C. Riley party?" he asked, half-turning his head but keeping his eyes on the road.

The two friends looked up.

"It looks like it," Dionne said.

Campbell laughed. "Mister Loverman I call him. Yeah, the women love him, throw their panties on stage at him. I had some things to do, but if you ladies are going, I'll probably go too."

"You need an invite, you know. You can't just walk in."

"Invite? You don't need an invite when your name's Campbell Clarke, trust me…"

Hoxton Square was a secluded little square just off Old Street on the edge of the City. Campbell dropped the ladies right outside the entrance to the Blue Note and watched them skip up the steps to the venue and enter, before circling the square to find somewhere to park.

"Yaow Clarkey! Wh'appen, star?"

Campbell beamed a big smile. He had been trying to figure out how to talk his way past the bouncers on the door without an invite, when the voice of one of the twins solved the problem. Ruffy and Tuffy were the bouncers for the night.

"Don't tell me, you've come to throw your panties at C. Riley as well," Ruffy teased.

Campbell told him to behave himself.

"I'm just passing through, y'know, just to see what all the fuss is about. And I hear that there's always 'nuff freeness at these record company parties."

"Yeah man, step right in?" Tuffy invited.

The party was filled with journalists (mostly women), record company people (mostly women) and a group of starry-eyed teenage girls who looked like they were fans, but could have been groupies. In one secluded corner of the club, with half a dozen mean-looking bodyguards forming a protective circle around him, C. Riley was chilling with his homies all of whom had a sexy looking woman on each knee. In the background, the pop star's latest single, *Grind Baby Grind*, was playing loudly.

Campbell soon found Dionne and Stella, who were sitting by a window, sipping coolly from their glasses of pink champagne.

"I told you I didn't need a ticket," Campbell said with a smile. "I've got contacts."

"In that case you can use your contacts to introduce us to C. Riley," Stella challenged.

Campbell looked across to the pop star, who was engaged in an intimate conversation with an attractive woman beside him.

"I think he's kinda busy right now...but I'll introduce you, don't worry, before the night's out you'll get to meet him."

"Good," Dionne said. "I'll get to tell him what I really think of his music."

"Hey, if I introduce you to him, I don't want you distressing him. My boy gets enough of that from journalists as it is...so where do you ladies hang out?"

"Here and there."

"I don't know that club, where is it?"

"Very funny. We go to lots of different places actually."

"Like for example."

"You'll find us any place where the music's fresh and exciting. Like, for example, Rampage, Ministry, Soul II Soul."

"My man Jazzie."

"So you know Soul II Soul?" she asked.

Campbell nodded. Just the other day he had driven Jazzie B from his mews offices in Camden Town to the BBC in White City. It wasn't that he knew him as his best friend, but Jazzie had given him his number and told him to call if he fancied looking around his recording studio.

At that moment, a burly black guy with dark sunglasses and a bomber jacket and black leather gloves came up to where they were sitting and addressed Dionne and Stella in a broad American accent.

"Ladies, Mr Riley would like to invite you both to join him at his table."

Dionne and Stella looked at each other with surprised but excited expressions.

"Wassup man?" Campbell addressed the bodyguard in his best yankee accent. "You know me and C. Riley are homies, so maybe I can just stroll back there with you guys?"

The bodyguard turned to Campbell with a mean,

unsmiling face. "The invitation is for two ladies only."

Campbell got the message. He could see there was no point in trying to get through to this gorilla. He had to sit back helplessly as Dionne and Stella got up to follow him. They barely had time to say "later" to Campbell before disappearing behind the human cordon around T Riley's entourage in the far corner.

Campbell got up to get a freebie beer from the bar, his attention focused on Dionne back there with C. Riley. She sat on one of his knees and Stella sat on the other. They looked as if they were enjoying everything. C. Riley was obviously enjoying it, because it looked like his eyes were undressing Dionne, like his lips were blowing kisses at her. Campbell felt a twinge of pain in his stomach as he watched the only woman on his mind entertaining and exciting the most dangerous ladykiller from the States. It's true, he was thinking, all you have to do is become a pop star and women will flock around you. He wished that C. Riley would simply disappear, while convincing himself that Dionne wasn't the kind of woman who lost her mind when she met a pop star. His heart was on fire and he watched C. Riley jealously, wishing that he were now in the singer's position. He could just imagine how good it must feel to be so close to Dionne. To be near enough to smell her, to touch her...

Then he realised what he was doing and snapped himself out of reverie. What was going on here? This woman was becoming an obsession and he seemed happy to let it happen. Never before had he felt like this about a woman. This shit had to be love.

59% of black men describe themselves as very confident that they know what their sexual partner wants from them during sex. 28% are fairly confident 10% are not very confident. 2% don't know and 1% are not at all confident.

A HANDFUL OF BUPPIES

She was on his mind. Good sense told him to forget her, but try as hard as he could, Campbell couldn't banish her from his thoughts. The things she said, the way she smoked, the expressions on her face. He could remember almost everything about her, but he couldn't remember exactly what she looked like and that was frustrating because he wanted to spend the night with her, right there in bed with him, even if it was only in his mind. For that though, he needed to have her picture vivid in his mind but the only things he could remember were the dark eyes, the pouting lips, the slight dimple on her cheek. The more he forced himself to conjure up an image of her, the less he could remember. The image he had was not complete and right now he wanted all of her, every bit of her, with him.

There were a few flashy cars parked outside the Owens' Hampstead home when Campbell arrived there the next evening, smartly dressed in a collarless green denim two-piece, with zip-pockets and rudebwoy sequins down the outside of the trouser leg. He pressed the doorbell. After a few moments, the door was opened by Valerie Owen. She seemed hardly surprised to see him there or by the fact that he had a huge bouquet of flowers in his hand.

"Hi Mrs O, your daughter left this in my car last night." He held up the engraved zippo lighter he had found on the back seat.

"Thank you," she said. "It was very kind of you to come all this way to return it."

There was an awkward silence for a moment as Valerie waited to see if there was anything else.

"Oh and these are for your daughter as well...for her birthday," Campbell said sheepishly.

"They're lovely," Valerie said, taking in their aroma. "How did you know?"

"Well, she mentioned it when I drove her last night...I've got a card as well..." he searched round in his pockets, before finding it and handing it to Valerie.

"Why don't you come in and give them to Dionne yourself?"

Campbell looked over her shoulder. He could see the guests gathered in the conservatory towards the back of the house, chatting away with drinks in their hands.

"Well...I'm not really invited..."

"Don't be silly," Valerie said, taking him by the arm and leading him in. "You must come in and have something to eat and there's lots to drink. I'm sure my daughter will be upset if you don't stay for at least one drink. Darling..." she called as they joined the guests, "another bunch of flowers for you."

Valerie Owen loved entertaining at home and her daughter's birthday was just another excuse to lay on a spread. Food was her business and quite naturally her parties always had the best. Campbell wandered through to the conservatory to join the other guests, the jerk chicken aroma wafting gently in the air as he passed by the kitchen.

The conservatory looked out over beautifully landscaped gardens. But from where Campbell was standing the grounds looked more like a never-ending park with trees and well-ordered shrubs and bushes lined up.

Dionne looked up from her conversation with a very

posh-sounding black guy who Campbell thought he recognised. Mrs Owen went to put the flowers in a vase.

"Oh, it's you…" was all Dionne could say when she saw Campbell. Then indicating the flowers, "You shouldn't have… How did you know it was my birthday?"

"You were chatting your business in my car yesterday, remember?"

"Don't you know it's rude to eavesdrop?"

"I could hardly avoid it in the car."

Dionne was only teasing. She said it was nice of him anyway. Campbell said it wasn't no big thing. "I couldn't hear that it was your birthday and not bring you anything."

"You'll have to tell me when it's your birthday…"

"Christmas Day," said Campbell, "you can't forget. Same day as Jesus."

"Yes, quite. Would you like a drink?"

Campbell said he would, a beer would be fine. "Come, let me introduce you to everyone."

It was a small but friendly gathering. There was Stella, of course. She smiled warmly at Campbell. "What happened to you last night? We looked for you before we went off to C. Riley's hotel. There was a party there, I thought you'd want to come. But you had already disappeared."

Campbell mumbled a reply.

Then there was Mike, who Campbell recognised as the man who had been with Dionne at the Ebony Club. Mike dressed and looked every bit like a city gent, the only difference being that he was black. He paused only briefly in his conversation with Michelle, a cousin of Dionne's, to acknowledge Campbell. They eyed each other suspiciously. Finally Dionne introduced him to Nick and Francis, a white couple, who were old friends of the family.

Campbell looked around the lounge, marvelling at everything. Valerie Owen liked to stuff her home with collectors' items as relentlessly as she enjoyed stuffing the stomachs of her guests with a never-ending round of meals.

Dionne returned with a glass of beer from the kitchen.

"This is just a little get-together," she said. "A few close friends. But of course you know that, don't you? Because you heard me talking on the phone yesterday."

Campbell made himself comfortable while Dionne returned to playing hostess with her other guests. Even though he had his back to her, he was secretly listening to every word she said and sneaking glimpses of her out of the corner of his eye. He was impressed with the way she dazzled her guests with her superlative hostessing and how clever she was at setting Mike up to fulfil her soft-voiced commands or even her unspoken needs with a little nagging, cajoling and seducing. "Darling, why don't you go through the collection and choose another CD to pop into the stereo... honey, if you're driving anywhere near the British Museum sometime this week, would you mind popping in and picking up one of those posters of the Benin mask? Oh you're such a dear."

Dionne seemed to be able to get men to do anything for her. In short, she was utterly, totally, one hundred percent mysteriously female.

Mike was speaking very loudly in his upper-class accent, which sounded more English than most English people. "Did I ever tell you about this Nigerian chap I was at Oxford with? Decent sort of fellow. He had some long unpronounceable African name, but of course we all knew him as Sam. Anyway, old Sam, poor chap, had the biggest lips in the entire college. I mean these weren't your normal African lips, these were absolutely extraordinary. I'm not kidding, they must have covered about a third of his face, so you can imagine how much we all used to tease him about it. Anyway, he kept saying, 'Look, you guys had better treat me with some respect, because one day I'm going to become a king. And of course we all laughed. We couldn't see him becoming king of anything with those lips. But believe it or not, one day his Uncle died and he became king of his tribe. The next thing we know, they sent down these four African chiefs, in full native ceremonial gear, to be his minders for the rest of his college days.

"Suddenly you couldn't just go up to see him in his rooms at any time any more, you had to make an appointment. Even me. And of course, with those warriors following him wherever he went, nobody ever dared to make fun of his lips again. But he never forgot about the teasing and when he returned to Nigeria for his coronation, he invited two of the guys who had teased him the most, on an all expenses paid trip to be his guests of honour at the ceremony. They were only too glad to take up his invitation because they thought they were going over to celebrate the coronation. You can imagine their surprise when they got there and realised that he was inviting them over to be publicly flogged. Ha ha ha."

From the man's concept of humour, Campbell concluded that his rival was nothing more than a coconut.

Campbell sat down on a chair staring at the TV and flicking the remote control until he found MTV. C. Riley's latest video, *Happiness Is A Honey With A Big Butt*. The video, featuring Riley dressed like Superfly in bell-bottoms, a thigh-length leather coat and a wide-brimmed hat with feathers, cavorting with a number of gyrating female rear ends in the back seat of his open-topped car, brought a smile to Campbell's face. Whatever he thought of C. Riley musically, he couldn't deny that the star had the most attractive women in his videos.

"Oh no, it's that C. Riley chap again," Mike announced loudly. "Isn't he just the most vulgar excuse for a pop star? I mean, the guy's got absolutely no talent, all he's doing is selling sex. It's so degrading."

Campbell looked over his shoulder to see Mike slip an

arm around Dionne's waist. He shifted uncomfortably in his seat, but not before he saw Dionne wriggle free from the embrace. Almost despite himself, Campbell found himself defending the pop star.

"He's no different from everybody else," he said. "Everybody uses sex to sell records nowadays."

Mike took up the challenge like a man on a mission.

"Yes, but most people know how to be subtle about it. C. Riley is just pornographic."

Campbell caught Dionne and Stella exchanging amused glances. He figured that here was a way of sliding into favour with Dionne. All he had to do was take C. Riley's defence.

"Don't you think that's a bit of exaggeration? All it is is a bit of bump and grind music. Ain't nothing wrong with that."

"I don't know how you can say that. Especially as a black man," Mike retorted. "Why does he have to sing about how large black women's behinds are? Do we really need to know. Can't you see that it's degrading?"

Campbell rode to the challenge.

"But he says that he's praising the way black women look, and that his songs are a celebration of black women."

"Poppycock! His obsession with black women's buttocks reminds me of those Nineteenth Century Europeans who went to uncivilised lengths to study it. Have you ever heard of the African slave Saartjie Baartman? She was more popularly known as the Hottentot Venus. Her chief appeal was her protruding fat buttocks. Nineteenth Century white society was so obsessed with a standard of beauty pretty much unattainable by them, that they used to display her on a platform in London and later in Paris, so that people could come and ogle at her as proof of black people's primitive and inferior nature. They even went so far as to dissect and preserve her genitalia in a jar after she died and they are still kept at the Musee de l'Homme in Paris. T Riley is just playing to that kind of bigotry."

Book-learning had never been Campbell's strong point. He couldn't compete with Mike's facts, figures and history, nor the moral high ground of his argument. Far from being a coconut, Mike seemed to have his head screwed on, even if he did dampen the spirit of the party with his home truths. And Campbell might have conceded defeat and given Mike props if he hadn't caught the triumphant smile on his face.

"Okay Mike, you've made your point," Dionne interjected. "I think I speak for women everywhere when I say we all wish C. Riley's songs aimed a little higher than our behinds. But hey, it's time to eat. Mum's laid on a fabulous spread."

They sat down to a sumptuous Caribbean feast of jerk chicken, plantains, steamed snapper and ackee and sweet potatoes. Campbell enjoyed it so much that he got a sudden urge to study gourmet cooking so that he could eat like this every day of the week.

The discussion during the meal turned to Campbell. Though he felt completely relaxed meeting new people, talking about himself in front of this particular audience caused him genuine pain and discomfort. They all seemed so better educated, so much more cultured and from all accounts had seen a lot more of the world than he had. What interesting things could he say? But everyone was waiting for him to speak. They were genuinely interested in knowing who he was, what he did and how he had come to know Dionne. Particularly Mike. Even within her wide social circle, Campbell didn't seem like the type of man Dionne usually associated with.

"I'm a cab driver," Campbell said.

There was a resounding hush as the guests exchanged glances of 'did I hear right?'

"He's not just any old driver," Stella quipped. "His cab is more like a limousine actually."

"But it's basically the same t'ing still," Campbell insisted. People might as well know exactly who he was. He couldn't fool them anyway, not with Stella, Dionne and her mother knowing the truth. The other guests were bound to regard his job as very humble. He would just have to swallow some humble pie.

"That's really fascinating," Michelle said. "You must meet a lot of interesting people."

"Yeah…mostly, but you get some bumboclaats as well."

"Oh, so you're bi-lingual," Mike said, "you speak ethnic as well as English."

Campbell could tell a piss-take when he heard it and wasn't too happy about Mike's sense of humour.

"What's ethnic mean?" he asked, as cool as ice.

This Mike found hilarious and he laughed so much he almost choked on the morsel of food he was chewing. Mike didn't get Campbell's sense of humour either.

"Dee baby, why don't we go away at the end of this week. It's been such a long time since we spent a whole weekend together," Mike suggested. It was the wee hours and by now, all but one of the other guests had already departed. Mike stood on the doorstep, talking in hushed tones, unable to tear himself away. He didn't want to go, but he had an early start.

"Go away? Where to? Brighton again?" Dionne had an ironic look on her face. She remembered the last time they spent a whole weekend together and the promises that were made then.

"No…better than Brighton. Why don't we fly to New York for the weekend? We could book the best suite in the Waldorf Astoria and do nothing more than sip champagne and look into each other's eyes."

"New York, eh? I'm sure it would be interesting, but…"

"But nothing. Let's just do it. I'll book the flight and the hotel in the morning."

"Wait Mike, hold it right there. I can't take all this sudden attention. Or have you forgotten your reservations about continuing this relationship?"

"Oh Dee baby, I thought we were past that. I've said how sorry I am. I just wasn't sure what I wanted. Now I do and I regret saying that. But it's all water under the bridge."

"You really think that you can slide in and out of relationships as easily as all that?"

"Well it's nothing to get uptight about is it?"

"Uptight? I'm not uptight. No, I'm not at all…I'm pretty calm. I'm just tired of all the bull, Mike. I want you to understand that and I don't think you do. I'm a big girl now and when you realise that you won't play my emotions like a yoyo…"

"But Dee, that's unfair. I made one little slip…"

"But that's all it takes sometimes, just one little slip."

"If we went to New York together, I'm sure I'd be able to straighten everything out easily."

"I'm sure you would. But that's a good reason for not going. You see Mike, I'm not sure about things between us any longer. I need time to think also. So let's take it easy, one step at a time. We're going to the cinema together tomorrow anyway, why don't we leave it at that for the moment."

The cinema! The words jolted Mike's memory. How could he have forgotten about accompanying Dionne to the film premier?

"Oh I forgot to tell you, Dee baby," he said in his sweetest voice, "I won't be able to make it tomorrow. The top man at the bank is flying in from Tokyo for only a few hours, and I've got to meet him. It was a last minute thing. No warning in advance. You know how difficult things can be at the bank. It's a three line whip, the only excuse that will be accepted for not being there is death."

Dionne sighed. "So what's new?" She turned to go back into the house. She was too tired to even be bothered. "You go ahead, Mike. Do what you've got to do. I'm going anyway, I've already got the invites. I intend to enjoy myself. I'm sure I won't have any trouble finding someone suitable to go with. There are bound to be lots of offers. Okay, see ya."

"Dee baby, I'll make it up to you. I promise I will." Mike called after her but he knew how headstrong she could be and she wanted him to leave. He really didn't want to go home, not while Campbell Clarke was still in the house. But he had no choice. *Doesn't this cab driver know when he's overstayed his welcome?*

Campbell, meanwhile, was a determined man and prepared to stay in Valerie Owen's house to the bitter end if necessary. He just didn't want to leave before Mike Phillips.

Back in the house, Mrs Owen and Campbell were engaged in a lively conversation on hypocritical Labour MPs in the dining room.

"I can well understand that Harriet Harman wants to send her son to a better school than the rest of the population," she was saying. "Let's face it, education is the single most important thing that divides the haves from the have-nots, the rich from the poor. With a little education, the sky is the limit—no, outer space is the limit. Every child deserves a chance to get an education, yet as far as our children are concerned, the state schools are not doing their job."

Campbell said he couldn't agree more, his school experience was a case in point.

"When they should be teaching our children how to deal with the real world waiting for them outside the school gates, they're still trying to teach them how to read and write. I think it's a disgrace."

"So why doesn't your government do something about it?" asked Campbell.

"Look, at the end of the day, most of the Tory voters are white people. My success in Brent was an exception to the rule, but everywhere else—what they call 'Tory heartland' is really the white man's heartland, where the voters will open all doors for you except the one you want to go through. Quite frankly, you couldn't convince any of those voters to increase taxes for state schools because their kids go to private schools and, to them, state schools translate as black schools. They're not interested in paying more taxes for a lot of black kids to go to school. Why should they be, their children don't attend those schools."

"So what you're saying is that we're always going to get the worst education, no matter what. Nothing changes."

"No, I'm not saying that. When black parents start making demands for their children's education, you'll see an improvement. Because if the teachers they've got at the moment can't do the job of teaching our kids, let's get rid of them and bring in more black teachers. Teachers who know what our children are really going to face out there in the world. In the absence of that, we've got to educate our kids ourselves."

"Easier said than done, Mrs O. The school route is cool, but it's not for everybody."

"We can't afford not to do it, so we'd better do it. Education isn't some kind of mystical thing. Knowledge is easy to acquire. It's out there for the taking. I had to educate myself, you know. Yes, m'dear. I married at sixteen and came from Jamaica with my husband in the late sixties. I didn't have anything more than a basic school qualification. And when my husband died suddenly, I had to bring up a daughter on my own. And the first thing I did was get my education. I worked days and studied at home by nights on

71

a correspondence course. I learned everything there was to learn about the food business. You could say I became an expert. Then I started my business, because I had learned that the secret to your success in this game of life is money equals happiness. Once you've mastered that important rule, you are in for a nice ride. Remember this: There's a fool born every morning. Try not to be one of them."

Dionne joined them, a miserable look on her face.

"Problems, darling?"

"Just the usual Mr Phillips problem," she said flopping down on a chair. "Mum, if he calls later, just tell him I'm not here."

"I don't know why you let him get to you like that, dear."

"Mum, please…I don't want to talk about it. He's always got some excuse…His boss is flying in, he's got to meet him."

Mrs Owen turned to Campbell. "Young love, you know?" She smiled a knowing smile, which Campbell returned rather sheepishly. Just then a thought struck Dionne.

"By the way Campbell, what are you doing tomorrow evening?"

"Nothing I couldn't get out of, why?"

"How would you like to escort me to the premiere of the new Othello film?"

Campbell beamed a wide smile. "Othello? Yeah, why not," he said calmly doing his utmost to restrain his leaping heart.

"That's settled then. Pick me up at seven."

With that Dionne yawned daintily and said that it had been a long, hard day. Campbell stood up at the same time and looking at his watch said that he had been there too long already. The time was almost three o'clock in the morning. He gave Dionne his best wishes for the rest of the year and thanked Mrs Owen for an enlightening discussion and said that he looked forward to the next one.

"So do I," Valerie Owen said with a warm smile. She followed him to the front door. "Drive safely now."

Campbell could hardly jump into the Jag fast enough.

"Yes!" he exclaimed in triumph with a raised fist. He had got a result.

Nobody had to tell Campbell to be on time for his date with Dionne Owen. In fact he was there early and parked a little distance from the Owen house, watching the minutes tick away on the car clock. He had pulled out his favourite suit for this one, the collarless dark-grey mohair job. Its elegant lines always showed off the best of his well-toned body. He had even taken time out to go to Dad's barber shop in Hoxton for a trim. And afterwards he had splashed more than a touch of his Ladykiller cologne which, he was assured by the Harrods sales person who sold it to him, no woman could resist. He wanted to make an impression.

Mrs Owen opened the door when he pressed the doorbell. She, at least, was impressed.

"My goodness Campbell, I thought you were going to see a film, you look like you're dressed to meet the Prime Minister."

"Well you know me, Mrs O, I'm ruling nothing in and ruling nothing out."

"Dionne darling, your carriage awaits you!"

Dionne called back down from upstairs, saying she wasn't ready. It took her another twenty minutes in fact. She came down finally.

"You're early," was the first thing she said when she came down the stairs looking magnificent in a sequinned black dress that dropped to above her knee.

"You mean you're late," Campbell smiled.

"Whatever. It's a lady's prerogative."

73

There was nothing Campbell could add to that, so they started making tracks.

"You youngsters have a good time," Mrs Owen called after. "And Campbell, take care of my daughter."

Campbell assured her that he would, then held the front passenger door of the Jaguar open for Dionne to climb in.

"You like Al Green, if I remember?" he asked when he was behind the steering wheel.

Dionne smiled.

Campbell slipped a tape on and the car was filled with *Love and Happiness*. With a roar of the engine, he pulled out, heading towards the West End.

"Are you sure we can make it in time. We've only got half an hour."

It was going to be tight, but Campbell was confident that it was possible. Especially at this time of the evening when there wasn't so much traffic."

"So what's this Othello film all about?"

"You must know the play. Othello, by Shakespeare."

"Oh that Othello, sure I do…he was a black general wasn't he? Married a white woman and ended up killing her at the end didn't he?"

"It's the first time a black actor has played Othello on film, can you believe that? After all these years. Laurence Fishburne is playing Othello. He's such a gorgeous actor. He's supposed to be there tonight as well."

"Hang on a second, is this the reason we're going to this film, because you've got a crush on the star?"

"No, of course not. It's supposed to be really good."

"Are you sure?" Campbell teased. "Because I'm not too crazy about the idea of sitting watching some handsome actor all evening. That's not the kinda guy I am."

Dionne laughed and assured him that it would be worthwhile going to see the film with or without Larry Fishburne. Campbell said he was happy as long as there

74

was going to be lots of action in the film: that was the kind of film he liked.

"So why do you think he changed his name? From Larry to Laurence. 'Cause when I saw him in *Boyz N The Hood*, he was definitely Larry Fishburne in those days."

"I expect it's because he got older. Larry sounds so young, don't you think."

"Well, what I think is that he probably got tired of being the only black man on the planet called Larry. Bwoy, if that was my name I would change it also. Quick time."

There was no mistaking the resemblance between Valerie and her daughter. They shared the same sugary almond eyes and angular cheekbones, the same elegance and charm. In fact, they looked more like sisters. And just like her mother, Dionne was certainly not afraid to get what she wanted in life.

"A lot of people say that we look like sisters," Dionne agreed when Campbell mentioned it. But mum doesn't like to hear that and is always reminding me that she's not my sister, that she's my mother and that I have to respect her because of that. We don't always see eye-to-eye. She thinks that I'm too much of a playgirl and that I can't stand up on my own two feet. You know how old-fashioned mothers can be. The thing we fall out most about is the men I bring home. She says I should have better things to do with my time than flitting from lover to lover, looking for that elusive 'perfect mate', or 'special someone'. And she's right too. I wish I was like her. I wish I could run my own company or run for Parliament and all those things, but that's not me. Mum tried to teach me to take over the running of the company, but even she's given up. I'm hopeless at it. You don't know how hard it is to be my mother's daughter, following in her footsteps. Maybe some day I'll discover my vocation in life, but at the moment I'm just trying to find myself. Do you know what I mean?"

Campbell nodded. He knew exactly what she meant. "What you need in your life is a good man," he told her. "I don't mean just any man, but a man who's going to be there for you, go through things with you and share things with you. Believe me, if you find the right man who can inspire you, you can do anything. Anything. Trust me."

Dionne sighed. "Maybe."

"You never know," Campbell smiled, "you might have found him already."

He wanted to play it cool. He had to play it cool, because he wasn't too sure how Dionne would take it if he told her how he really felt. How much he adored her. Would she think him odd for falling for someone he hardly knew? Supposing she rejected him and thought him mad for it? Stuff all the learning to say 'no', he thought, he too wanted the warmth and tenderness of romance. It wasn't his fault that the feelings had come over him so quickly in such a short time. If he waited years he was going to feel the same way, he knew he was. It wasn't going to change, so might as well get it over and done with now.

He knew what he had to say, he had chatted up women a thousand times, but it was coming like this was the biggest decision in his life. Why did it feel like such a big deal to tell her that she had featured in the first dream he could remember for years the previous night. He wanted to tell her so many things. How was he supposed to keep control of his thoughts when all his soul was ablaze with longing for her?

"So what do you think about me?"

So this was it. She had sensed that it was something of the sort, but she had hoped that it wasn't. It wasn't the first time she had heard that line but she had heard better ones. He would need much better lyrics than that, she was thinking.

"What do you mean, what do I think of you?"

"Just generally."

"I think you're very nice, Campbell. You're a good driver...reliable. I think you're alright. What more can I say?"

"I don't know, but if you want to say more, go ahead."

"But there's nothing to say."

"You like talking to me?"

"Yes...the few chats we've had..."

"I guess you know that I'm crazy about you?"

She looked at him hard.

"Look, no offence," Dionne said, "but we're just going out for the evening. Don't flatter yourself into thinking that going to the cinema together equals going to bed together."

"I wasn't thinking that at all."

"Good. Then we understand each other. This is just a date, right?"

"Right. But I just wanted you to know. I'm sure that loads of men tell you that they fancy you, and I can understand that because you're definitely fanciable. And I can't explain what's going on inside of me right now, but I know you caused it."

"This is beginning to sound like your chat-up line."

"Not really. It's just a way of telling you how I feel."

"I already know how you feel, you're feeling horny. It's written all over your face."

"Well if you're so good at reading my face, I'm sure you can see that 'I'm crazy about you' is also written all over my face."

" 'I'm crazy about you', 'I'm feeling horny' and 'my place or yours'. It's all there, and not necessarily in that order."

"Look Dionne, I can't deny that if you said 'Cam, let's go to bed after the movie', I wouldn't say 'no'. But you can't blame me for that. After all, you're a woman and I'm a man."

"And that's just the problem. A man never learns to say

77

'no'. Let me give it to you straight, Campbell. Good girls never ask for it and a gentlemen never suggests it. Now I know I'm a good girl, the question is are you a gentleman?"

"That depends. How do good girls and gentlemen ever get it on?"

"It comes by itself. It's a spiritual thing."

"But that's what I'm talking about when I say I'm crazy about you. It's not me saying that, it's coming from deep within my soul. Maybe my soul can get with your soul and maybe go out together again sometime."

"Soul to soul?"

"My man Jazzie B again."

"Okay, but let's keep it like that, shall we?"

Easier said than done. Campbell was unable to take his mind off her as he drove. Even though it seemed like he wasn't going to get a squeeze, he still refused to believe that his feelings were a lost cause, that there could never be anything between him and Dionne. Furthermore, he was looking for more than a squeeze and had visions in his mind of something much more permanent, frame by frame images of the future, their children—a boy and a girl, the things they would do together, the places they would go. All day long he had wanted to talk to her and it had been with the greatest self-restraint that he stopped himself from picking up the phone every fifteen minutes to call her and say "let's get married today", because the way he felt he wanted to go and get a preacher. If things were only that simple.

Campbell made speedy progress and they got to the West End with fifteen minutes to go before the start of the premier. The next problem though, was finding somewhere to park. It seemed like there wasn't a single parking space in the whole area. At least not one large enough to allow a Jag to ease in. Campbell spent the next ten minutes circling Shaftesbury Avenue, Covent Garden and Soho, trying to slot himself in without success. Fortunately, he remembered the little alley—way off St Martin's Lane where he had parked many times before.

"I'll remember this spot for future reference," Dionne said, impressed, as they hurried across Charing Cross Road, towards the cinema.

"That's one of the little benefits of driving around all day, you get to know all the back streets and the little spots where you can park without getting a ticket. I can show you a lot of good spots in London. Believe."

There was still a large crowd outside the cinema when they arrived, though most of the cinemagoers were already seated inside. Just as they were about to go in, Campbell heard someone call, "Dee, baby!"

Dionne spun around and stood facing the man.

"Mike," she said flatly.

"Dee baby, I managed to get here after all. I got out of the meeting with my boss. I know how much tonight means to you, so I'm here."

"It's too late."

Mike looked flustered but just kept grinning. He couldn't understand what she was saying.

"I said it's too late. I've already got someone to go with," said Dionne, gesturing towards Campbell. "The last thing you said last night was for me to enjoy myself. That's what I'm doing, but without you. Now if you don't mind, we're in a hurry."

Mike did mind.

"I know you're angry at me, but this isn't the way to get back at me. If we've got a problem, let's talk about it."

At this point Campbell stepped in. "Man, you heard the lady."

But to his surprise Mike simply ignored him.

"So you're dating the chauffeur?" he asked Dionne.

The man definitely deserved a smack for that, thought

Campbell. But how could he justify it. It was true after all.

"Oh grow up," Dionne retorted, pushing her way past him followed by Campbell, who gave the spurned lover one last sinister look.

"Tickets, tickets…you wanna buy a ticket, mate?"

Mike spun around to face the ticket tout. "Yes, I'd like a ticket, how much?"

"Just fifty quid, mate."

"Fifty quid!"

"Take it or leave it, mate. Plenty other customers."

Mike took it. It was his only chance.

Inside the cinema, Dionne and Campbell fumbled their way to their seats in the dark and settled down just as the opening credits finished rolling. Campbell was looking forward to the film until the actors started speaking. *Damn!* He forgot, Shakespeare was all in that funny language.

"Can you understand what they're saying?" he whispered to Dionne beside him.

"Shhhh! It's Shakespeare. You've got to concentrate."

So Campbell did just that for the first fifteen minutes, but his mind quickly started drifting. Unable to make head or tail of all this talk about 'Moors', he leaned back in his seat and with his heart beating, decided to make his move. It was so quietly done, so slowly done, that Dionne didn't even notice a thing when he took her hand in his and squeezed it gently. But wait, her hand was rough, hairy! He turned his head and shot her a look of horror, only to find himself facing Mike Phillips' irritated face. Both men tore their locked hands away in revulsion. Mike was sitting in the seat to the other side of her, having crept up the aisle in the darkness after the show had begun.

Campbell glared at him for a moment, before leaning back in his seat and turning his attention back to the silver screen ahead. But his mind was totally on Mike. This man was seriously cramping his style.

The film ended to rapturous applause from the audience. The lights came on and the celebrity guests present at the screening took a bow. To Dionne's disappointment, there was no sign of Laurence Fishburne, the star of the film. Campbell joked that Fishburne must have guessed that she'd be looking out for him and therefore decided to stay at home. From the look on Mike's face he didn't think that was funny. He didn't think it was funny at all. In fact, he thought it was a banal comment, and said as much. The two men escorted Dionne out of the cinema, one on either side of her. Both vying for her attention.

"It's such a beautiful evening. You know what I'd like to do?" Dionne said when they stood outside the cinema, speaking to neither man in particular. "I'd like an ice cream. Why don't we go to Haagen Dazs?"

Campbell was the first one to say yes, that was a good idea. But it was Mike who took her by the waist and led her towards the ice cream bar at the corner of the Square.

"Does *he* have to come too?" Mike asked.

"Of course he does. *He* was the one I came out with tonight, remember."

Mike sighed wearily. That was all he could do.

They sat with an ice cream each at a window table in the corner of the crowded bar. Even though it was almost midnight, a queue of people eager for a night-time sundae had begun to form outside.

"I do wish they wouldn't keep bringing these Americans over to play roles meant for English actors," Mike was saying. "I mean, Fishburne was alright and everything, but there are plenty of actors over here who could have done that role better. There's something too English about Shakespeare that the Americans just can't grasp."

"Othello is such a sad story," Dionne said, staring thoughtfully down at her chocolate ice. "All the way through I just wanted to scream at him for not trusting his wife."

"But of course that's the whole point of the tragedy, it shows human weakness. Jealousy is one of those deadly sins and it drove him to a blind, murderous rage. If Desdemona wasn't pure and innocent, it would hardly be a tragedy."

Campbell cringed as his rival expounded confidently about the film. Mike at least must have known what was going on.

"But that kind of blind rage is something you just don't find with women. What is it about men that they would rather listen to their friends before talking to their women?"

"Oh be fair, Dee baby, Iago was, after all, a hostile witness. If Iago was a true friend to Othello he wouldn't have told him lies about his wife having affairs. And at the end of the day, you've got to consider the exceptional circumstances Othello found himself in. You've got to remember that he was a Moor, the one black man around. He was a stranger in a foreign city, unfamiliar with the ways of the Italians and he was vulnerable. I can quite understand why he believed that. What do you think, Cannibal?" he said turning to Campbell with a cynical grin.

"The name's Campbell...Anyway, what I think is that this Shakespeare guy wrote the book because he didn't want any white women with a touch of jungle fever going after any black men. It's a warning to white women, you go after a black man and here's what's gonna happen to you. It's a classic case of fear of a black penis."

That was funny enough to make Dionne laugh. Mike merely grimaced and gave Dionne a look of 'where did you pick up this guy?' before explaining to Campbell condescendingly that *Othello* was not a book, but a play. "There is a difference, you know."

"Not in the part of town I come from there ain't."

Campbell was tired of feeling embarrassed that he

wasn't as clever and cultured as Dionne's friends. Tired of thinking that what he had to say sounded boring compared to all the exciting things they had done and talked about. Now he was going on the attack. He had nothing to be ashamed about.

"And what part of town may I ask is that?" Mike sneered.

"The loudest and proudest part of town—Hackney."

"Otherwise known as the ghetto." Mike was not too impressed.

"Call it what you wanna call it."

"In that case I will. I'll call it Crack City, Land of Dope and Glory, No Man's Land, Mugger's Paradise. They say the brightest hope in Hackney is the road leading to Islington."

"Hackney's not really that bad, is it Campbell?" Dionne asked with interest.

"It's not bad at all. It's all good. It's just that some people are tired of being the ones who have to do without a car, without a house, without the clothes, without the girl. I'm tired of all that stuff too. Look at me man, I've had a hard life. It ain't made-up, it's real. I want you to know that."

"Oh my heart bleeds for you."

"I don't need your sympathy, 'cause I can take care of myself and I'm going to get mine."

"And how are you going to do that, by mugging some old lady, or by selling crack to school children."

That was too much. Campbell stood up angrily, his fists at the ready. Mike would have already been nursing a fat lip if it wasn't for the fact that Campbell was sure that he would regret throwing the first punch. How would that look to Dionne? Something told him that it wouldn't go down too well with her and that would be playing straight into Mike Phillips' hands.

"If you're going to start fighting, I'll leave you both to it and go home," Dionne suggested. They were both behaving like children. Even though Mike was out of order, there was no reason for Campbell to resort to violence at the slightest provocation. "Mike, why do you have to be so rude?"

"What have I said? What have I done?" he protested.

"You know very well," Dionne said. "You've been going out of your way to be disagreeable all evening for some reason."

"Look, it was just a joke. Really it was. Look man, chill out. Sit down. I apologise okay, I think you misunderstood. Seriously, how are you going to 'get yours'?"

Campbell's chest was still rising up and down and his adrenaline was rushing, but it felt like he had been outplayed and the tables had turned on him. Now he wondered whether he had over-reacted. He didn't like being made a fool of, but he had to win the battle of words, otherwise Dionne might lose respect for him. If necessary he would sit there all night. Anything to avoid giving Mike the chance to be alone with Dionne.

"I said, how do you intend to get yours?"

"Don't worry yourself about that." Campbell knew what he wanted and was prepared to go through countless miseries trying to get it. "I've got a plan, a little strategy to start making some money."

"Ahhh, a plan. A little strategy. You see, that's the difference between you and me. You've got a little strategy from which it follows you'll get a little money. Me on the other hand, I don't bother with little strategies. I see the big picture, because that's where the big money is. I'm not thinking about millions, I'm talking billions. But don't let that stop you. You go ahead with your little strategies and I'll carry on with my big plans. We'll see which one of us will be rich and which one of us won't."

"And we'll see which one of us will suffer a stroke and which one of us won't. King-size plans usually come with king-size high blood pressure."

"I'll take care of that with my king-size medical insurance. No problem."

"You think that money can get you everything, but you're wrong." Campbell couldn't believe the ignorance of the man.

"That shows how naive you are about the world. Have you ever heard the phrase, 'money is king'?"

"Have you ever read your Bible to know that God is king?"

"In this day and age, even God would have to admit that more people worship money than worship Him."

"I don't know about you, but the people I know don't worship money, all they want is a little happiness in their lives. But you can have all the money and power in the world and you still won't find happiness. Happiness is finding the woman of your dreams and discovering that you're the man of her dreams. All the money in the world couldn't buy that."

"Look at it this way, without money, there isn't going to be any happiness, because the woman of your dreams isn't dreaming of hardship. It follows that the more money you have, the more likely you are of becoming the man of her dreams."

Dionne, who had been sitting quietly throughout the constant volleying back and forth could not contain herself any longer.

"What a load of nonsense. What are you both talking about?"

"But it's true," Mike insisted. "Would you marry a pauper?"

Dionne could feel herself getting dragged into it when she would rather stay out. Mike repeated his question.

"Of course not. But that's not the point."

That was exactly the point Mike said, with a victorious

smile.

"You see Campby, Dionne is a practical sort of woman and will always choose a husband who fulfils her needs for stability and respect in the eyes of the community and a husband who can keep her in the lifestyle that she's accustomed to. Isn't that so, honey?" Mike took her hand and caressed it gently. Dionne saw his game and snatched her hand back.

"Mike, you don't know what I want or what I don't want. Please, don't presume. I'm not stupid enough to go looking for a man who is broke, but it doesn't mean that money is my highest priority in a relationship. Devotion is more important than money. The man I marry will be devoted to me and committed to me. I don't need a man to support me. As long as he's able to support himself in the lifestyle that I'm accustomed to, I'll be happy to marry him. But he's got to be someone intelligent who I can have a conversation about anything with. Someone who's easygoing in a relationship that's easy and stress free. But every situation and every person is different, so who knows, I might meet someone with no money and fall madly in love."

"I don't think so somehow," Mike said with a wry smile. "How about you, Camp? What kind of woman do you want to marry?"

Campbell thought about it for a long moment before answering.

"I'm looking for a real partner, not just in love, but in life. Someone who's fun-loving with brains and common-sense, who looks good and cares about herself and others. A woman who works out quite often and is in shape. A woman that loves kids and wants to have two with me. A woman with kids already is also fine. A relationship to me is totally equal. She should be prepared to be a partner. 'Cause I've seen too many men use women and I've seen just the reverse: men hurt by women who seemed to just get what they want and not give anything back.

"I'm a romantic and when I find that special someone, that woman who is willing to teach this guy how to love and be loved, I'll ask her to marry me. And she won't care whether I'm the richest man in the world or not. The road may be rough sometimes, but I'll take care of her. We may not have a cent to pay the rent, but we're going to make it. I know we will. We may have to eat rice every day, but we'll make it. I know we will. Even if we don't have a home to call our own."

An unexpected drizzle had dampened the summer night.

"Look, I've got the Ferrari in the car park on the other side of the square," Mike was saying as they stepped out of the Haagen Dazs into the swarm of people rushing for the last underground train.

"I'll be alright, thank you," Dionne said. "Campbell is driving me home."

"Oh come on, Dee baby, I've said I'm sorry. Let's forget all this. I'll give the man a tenner for his troubles and I'll take you home."

"Mike, you keep forgetting that you cancelled tonight, remember? You ruled yourself out. Why isn't that getting through to you?"

Mike wasn't easily put off and insisted on following Campbell and Dionne all the way to their car.

The alleyway was dark and quiet when they arrived and apart from Campbell's Jaguar parked half way up, empty. Campbell's heart started pounding fast and then sunk deep as he saw first what looked like a notice plastered on the windscreen, and then the familiar yellow of the wheelclamp gripping his rear wheel.

"Oh I see, this is your ride home is it?" Mike could not contain his amusement.

Campbell cursed under his breath and turned to Dionne with a bemused look on his face. He had parked there plenty of times before and never had so much as a ticket. They couldn't clamp him.

"But they have," Dionne assured him. There was no point in arguing with the fact. While Mike stood back with a big smile, Campbell pulled out his mobile and dialled the appropriate number and after a couple of minutes of discussion snapped shut the phone with a crestfallen expression.

"It's going to take them an hour to get here."

Dionne shivered.

"Dee baby, there's no point in standing here. Come on, let me take you home." Mike put an affectionate arm around her waist. Dionne looked at Campbell with a helpless expression. There was no point in both of them waiting for the car.

"Why don't you call me tomorrow—not too early—and we'll arrange to meet up or something. Do you have the time?"

"Maybe. I'll call you."

"Yes, do that."

She turned and accompanied Mike to his Ferrari.

13% of black men men (who are not virgins) say they have sex less than once a month. 5% say they are currently celibate (involuntarily).

NO WEDDINGS NO FUNERALS

"Oh yeesss…oohhhhh, yeeeeeeessssss…now bite it…yessss, bite it again…harder, harder…oh yesssss…ooooohhh yesss."

Campbell felt revolted. It was the third time in a week that he had been called to pick up the white dude from his house in Fulham, and each time it was the same thing. He was a handsome looking white guy in his late twenties or early thirties, it was difficult to tell because he never once removed his wraparound darkers, with tanned skin and a trendy haircut. On all three occasions, he had asked to be driven to Paddington and when they got there would get Campbell to drive slowly until he found what he was looking for. He didn't just want any prostitute, but had a penchant for big black women with rubbery lips. Then he would get Campbell to drive up and down some of the residential streets in Bayswater even though it was still early evening, while he got a blowjob. For the next fifteen minutes Campbell would try and keep his mind on the road, with a pained expression on his face, while the dude in the back was screaming with ecstacy.

"Oh   baaaaaby…yesssss…that's   good,   that's goooooooood. Oh yesssss, harder, faster, deeper…here I come baby…take it all…here I come…I'm coming, I'm coming, I'm coming, I'm coming…I'M COOOOOOMIIIIIIING!"

Then they would return to Paddington. The prostitute would get paid and Campbell would drive back to Fulham without a word from his passenger.

He glanced in his rearview mirror as he hit the Fulham Road. Despite the sunglasses, he couldn't help thinking he had seen the guy somewhere before.

As soon as he had dropped the man off, Campbell hit the switch operating the windows and let some air in. *Damn!* Why did he have to drive a prostitute around in his car. It was pure slackness to book a cab and use it as a pussy machine, but he needed his job more than he needed to kick the dude's ass. As he drove back into town, he could smell the musty odour of stale sex in the car. He pulled out a can of air freshener from the glove compartment and sprayed the interior until he could barely breath. *Why do people have to do stuff like that in other people's cars?* "The customer is always right," Louie was always telling him. "You take them wherever they want to go do whatever they want…they're ALWAYS right." He kissed his teeth angrily. Now he would have to pull into a petrol station to wipe any icky off the back seat. *Damn!* He looked at his watch. *Damn!* He would have to be quick if he wanted to reach the sauna before closing time. He had just enough time to hold a fresh before picking Dionne up. He had called her up earlier and they had agreed to go out. Despite the disastrous ending to their night at the cinema she had enjoyed his company and had felt embarrassed by Mike's treatment of him. This would more than make up for that.

As always, the sauna was steaming. Mikey and Bucky, two young regulars, stepped into the cubicle, hailed everybody up and punched fists with the twins. Mikey and Bucky were sound men who also ran one of the most popular junglist pirates on the airwaves. Only a few know what it is to hold a mike like a jewelled sceptre and chat lyrics like your life depended on it. Only a few can really kick a dance by chanting into the reverberating baton, with a boy behind them manipulating a Technics turntable—dusting vinyl, moving the LP with middle and forefinger to and fro, finding the spot, backing it up, finding the spot and then letting it spin and all—to a rowdy reception of simulated gun shots from an excited audience. Only a few know how to really rock da house and, by all accounts, Mikey and Bucky knew.

"So what happened with the session in Brixton?"

"We wrecked the show fe real," Bucky bragged and boasted. "With some real true hardcore stuff...all the other sounds had to bow down. We was dropping special after special after special..."

"That's the only way to do it," Mikey agreed. "All these new deejays just wanna get paid."

"Without paying their dues."

"What do they know about where the music's coming from? It ain't gotta sell a million copies as long as you know it's slamming and the underground knows. To be really different as a deejay you've got to be heartical."

"Yeah, 'cause that's the difference between us and them, when we believe in a record, we lean on it...plant it in people's ears, let them hear. But if I can't feel it, I won't play it."

Mark came into the sauna then, a stocky redskin youth with a pencil thin moustache, close cropped hair. Mark was a barrister who worked out of chambers in Holborn, but always tried to make it up to the sauna sessions at least once a week if he wasn't in court. A graduate from the school of hard knocks, Mark was born on the wrong side of the tracks, went to the wrong schools and was brought up the rough way. But he was one of those rare brothas who knew he could when everyone and everything around him told him he couldn't. And he was proud of what he had achieved, because, like he often liked to remind people, "I had to fight for mine and get myself heard by all the right people." He might wear a pinstripe suit to work and have a voice which made him sound like a toff, but dressed in his swimming trunks in the steaming sauna, he was just one of the fellas. The guys made space for him. Mark squeezed in beside Trevor, greeting him with a smile.

"…A white guy comes up to a black guy and says, 'Why do you black guys like holding your willies so much?' The black guy says to the white, 'Because you took everything else from us, so we're just checking to make sure we still have that—it's the only thing we have left. Then the white guy turns around and says, 'You've still got something left? In that case we ain't done with your ass yet'."

Fat Freddy was in the sauna also, reasoning about equal rights and justice and throwing in 'nuff ruffneck comedy too. From his corner in the cubicle, Campbell was taking it all in appreciatively, with the reverence that one brother can have for another, just kicking back as if he had been tight with the crew for years. There was nothing complex about it: sometimes they would drink a brew or two together, kick back together. Outside, some dressed in suits, while others wore Malcolm X teeshirts, baseball caps and the latest baggy denim jeans, but in the sauna they were all the same and lived by the unspoken maxim, 'all for one and one for all'.

Yes, with Black Man United, Campbell had his back well covered. Now all he had to do was watch his front, because, like Trevor was fond of saying, "I got your back Clarkey, but it's best to watch your front, 'cause it's the niggas in front who'll be pulling stunts."

"Don't you know that the fastest runner in the world is a black man? And the greatest boxers in the world are all black men who can lick you down in a minute. Look how many things that black is best in, dancing, fashion, style, lovemaking —it's true. And who says that black people can't swim? What about that gal who comes to the pool with her mother first thing every morning, swimming like she's going to be representing England in the next Olympics? Ain't nothing wrong with her. Her bones don't seem to be too heavy to me. That's the only reason they want us in this country anyway—so that we can bring back all kinds of gold medals for them and they can tease the other European countries by chanting, 'Our nigger's better than your nigger!' Anything to make Britain great again. Skeen? You nuh see, when a country does well in the Olympics, its stock market goes up and everybody prospers. That's why all these black footballers shouldn't bother about getting into the English team. They're wasting their time, they're better off playing for their home teams in the Caribbean or Africa, instead of trying to get into a team where they're not appreciated. Skeen? But that's black people for you. The five most expensive players in British soccer are black, but they're not getting props, yet they'll bend over backwards to be in the white man's team...Collymore should be representing and so should Cole, Ince and Ferdinand, but they can't even get in the squad! And as for Asprilla, so what if he's headbutted an opponent? He's still one of the best out there."

Fat Freddy was really on form, getting stuff off his chest that had been simmering for a while. Before long he was in another discussion:

"'Ooman ah run t'ings...internationally. Skeen? Watch'a nuh, the Prime Minister may be a man, but behind every Prime Minister, there's a 'ooman running the country. No dat me ah read inna the papers the other day? The black 'ooman ah run t'ings. An' dem earning so good dem caan find a man fe satisfy dem. Yeah man, the 'ooman dem ain't staying at home no more. That's why pussy ain't what it used to be. I mean, let's face it, it ain't like the old days. Back in the old days when you got some real pussy it was really something. You went home thinking about it for weeks or even months. The gal dem nowadays don't care how good the pussy is as long as they're controlling a good dick. No, take it from me, you couldn't beat that old-time pussy…"

Fat Freddy didn't mean to cause offence. When he talked like this it was just the way they all acted when they were chilling in the sauna, jesting with each other in the bi-lingual mix of Jamaican patois and cockney, the unofficial language of the street. These were just some of the ways they joked with their spars when their women weren't around. The sauna was one of those places where black men could come together and express themselves, while steaming off the stress of trying to make a living in Babylon.

On the top bench opposite Fat Freddy, Mikey and Bucky were discussing the merits or otherwise of a new record.

"You think it's wack?"

"Wick-wick-wack," Mikey replied. "It's too fast and the beat is tired. Now if you're talking about Biggie Smalls, that's a different story. That shit is straight-up dope. Anybody who knows any little thing about hip hop will buy three copies of that shit."

Over in another corner, an animated Sweetbwoy was appealing to the twins for sympathy, with his characteristically impish charm.

"She's trying to make out as if I kept my pickney a secret from her…I mean, how far can you go with a lie? How long would it last? Especially concerning children. I just ignore the stuff. 'Cause once you start denying, it just starts more shit."

"Yeah, life's a bitch," Ruffy empathised.

"That's something every man can relate to," Fat Freddy said as he prepared to leave the steaming cubicle. "Sometimes a black man's gotta be a bitch to survive. We're fighting for our manhood here."

Trevor came into the sauna in an ebullient mood. He had just won a big payout at the bookies and amid the congratulations from his friends, invited everyone to follow him across the road for a drink. The invitation was no sooner made than accepted and everybody filed out of the cubicle, got dressed and followed Trevor to the pub, where the drinks were indeed 'on him'. The conversations continued from where they had left off in the sauna, each man with a lager or a Dragon in hand. A few of the crew were standing by the pool table where a heated game was in progress, as a line of people looked on, waiting for their turn on the table. It looked as if Fat Freddy was about to give Sweetbwoy a beating. Meanwhile, Trevor and Campbell propped up the bar with a beer in each hand.

"You want another one?"

"Hey, take it easy Trev, you're going to spend that money quick-time if you're not careful."

"Careful? You don't worry about me. Money's supposed to be spent. Hey Mr Barman…another Dragon for my bredrin."

Campbell thanked him and they clinked bottles in an informal toast.

"As a matter of fact, I was thinking of passing by Vivienne's, you know, surprise her…take her out for the evening. Maybe catch a film up West and then go for dinner or something. You fancy coming along?"

Campbell said he didn't think so. Vivienne was Trevor's long-suffering baby mother. Campbell was pleased to know that his friend still showed his sorry-ass face around there once in a while to treat her good. That relationship had been going on since they were teenagers and it looked like they were going to stay nominally together though thick and thin.

"Nah man, two's a party, three's a crowd. The last thing Vivienne wants is me hanging around when you finally decide to take her out."

But Trevor insisted that it wasn't a problem. He would

tell Vivienne to invite one of her girlfriends and they could make it a foursome. Campbell still shook his head.

"There you go again, man. Always trying to hook me up. Thanks, but no thanks."

"Are you sure man? Because Vivienne's got some criss friends, you know. You'll be grateful."

Still Campbell said no.

"You're not still on that no sex tip are you? Because don't think I didn't see you get off with that lawyer woman at the Ebony Club. So how was she?"

Campbell nodded with a grin on his face to indicate that it was pleasurable.

"So did you do the nasty?"

Campbell shrugged his shoulders. "As a matter of fact, yes."

Trevor let out a triumphant cry and slapped his friend on the back approvingly. "Yeah man. That was the best news I've had today. Even better than winning on the gee-gees. That's more like it, Clarkey. I could tell that you got laid, because you don't have that miserable look on your face you've been having over the last few weeks. Man, you were getting downright depressing to be with. Now, this is more like you, this is the Clarkey I know. All you needed was to get your end away, man, and start living again."

Campbell smiled shyly. "Well, you know how it is, a man's gotta do what a man's gotta do."

"So let's go out this evening then, if you're back in circulation. Vivienne's got this girlfriend…Tina…Man, she's got 'horny' written across her face. Trust me."

Campbell shook his head. Yes, he had got off with the lawyer woman, but that had only made him more determined to stay away from any other women. And anyway, he was so tired, he hadn't slept for two days. He wouldn't be any good to anyone.

Trevor said he'd let him off this time, but he wasn't going

to let him get away with all this staying away from women talk. Campbell shrugged. Soon, he hoped, he would be able to tell his spar about Dionne, but first he had to have something concrete to reveal.

Campbell was ready to hit the sack when he got home. That's what a long session in the sauna does. It was a good thing that Trevor had gone off on his date, because it meant that he had the bedsit to himself and if there was ever a time when he needed some peace and quiet, it was now. He didn't want to talk about women or think about them, he just wanted to sleep. Nevertheless, thoughts of Dionne preyed on his mind. He stripped to his boxer shorts, pulled out the mattress from the wardrobe and flopped down, exhausted.

It seemed like he was in a deep slumber, yet the insistent ring of his mobile soon penetrated Campbell's dreams. Still half-asleep, he fumbled around for the phone before finding it.

"Surprise!" a merry female voice greeted him down the line.

"Dionne?!" He could hardly believe it.

"Boy, you sound rough," Dionne giggled down the phone.

"Wha...What time is it?" he mumbled, still unsure of whether he was asleep or awake.

"It's not even eleven yet. Don't tell me it's past your bedtime already," she teased. "So what happened today? I thought you were going to call."

Now it was all beginning to register. Dionne had told him to call her, but he was still smarting from the way she left him when his car got clamped and didn't feel like calling.

"Anyway, I decided to call you. I was thinking of coming

over."

"Over? Where?"

"To see you. I want to make up for last night."

"What?!"

"You don't sound too happy about it."

"No, it's not that." *No, it definitely isn't that!* Campbell was only too eager for an opportunity to see her.

"Alone?"

"Of course I'm alone," she giggled.

"Well in that case..." Campbell cast a nervous glance around the room. Trevor's bedsit suddenly seemed a lot smaller, much more cluttered and untidier than he thought it was. Maybe he should tell her that he really wasn't in the mood for company. *Are you crazeeee?!*

"Come right over," he said.

No sooner had he snapped his phone shut than he was lighting incense—the one called *Love Supreme*—and vacuuming the carpet. He tidied up as best he could and to give the room the finishing touch, he switched off the overhead light and lit a couple of candles, giving the room a sensual ambience. The mood was right and pretty soon the time would be right.

Dionne arrived soon after with a twinkle in her eye and trailing a scent of Coco Chanel. Her smile seemed wider than Campbell remembered it and she carried a bottle of chilled champagne.

"Surprise!!" she giggled, tripping over her stiletto heels and falling unsteadily into Campbell's arms.

"You look magnificent," he said, admiring her slinky silk halterneck, "your face, your hair, the perfume you're wearing..."

Dionne giggled again. "You don't look so bad yourself," she complimented. It was true, Campbell looked and smelled as if he had just stepped out of the shower and into a new pair of slacks and a new white shirt.

99

"Welcome to my home," Campbell said, showing her in.

"It seems really cosy," she said, casting a tipsy gaze around the room. Then she waved the bottle in her hand. "Why don't you get a couple of glasses."

Campbell said that was a good idea and disappeared briefly into the kitchenette and returned a moment later with two glasses which he filled with champagne. Dionne had already made herself comfortable on the bed sofa. They clinked glasses.

"I guess I'd better start talking about why I'm here…" she began.

"No need…I know why you're here," Campbell said, sitting down beside her. "You've had a drink or two and now you're in the mood. I'm also in the mood."

"In the mood? I just came by to see how you were doing and maybe spend some time together."

Campbell smiled. He was prepared to go along with whatever she said, but when a man's got that feeling about a woman he *knows* what she wants.

"So here I am," he said. "Let's spend some time together…do anything you want to. I'm here and I'm all yours."

Dionne had had one or two drinks too many to get Campbell's drift.

"I came here just to talk really," she continued. "I've been at home all evening on my own and I just got this urge to go and visit a man. Do you know what I mean?"

"So what about Mike?" Campbell asked.

"What about Mike?"

"Oh, have you forgotten about him already?"

"No, I didn't say that."

"Well? What's his story?"

"He's highly sophisticated and he's intelligent. The perfect gentleman," Dionne said with a touch of irony.

Campbell nodded. He wanted to know more.

"He's a broker in the City," Dionne continued, "works for a big American company. Went to Oxford and all that."

Campbell shrugged his shoulders. He didn't want a CV. He wanted to know what Mike was really like and why Dionne bothered with him. "So are you two an item or something?"

"Or something..." Dionne said absent-mindedly.

"So he's your main squeeze?"

"Something like that."

"Pity…" Campbell heard himself say.

"Oh, he's alright," she said with a deep sigh. "I suppose I'm a bit hard on him sometimes."

"No, not at all," Campbell said quickly. "He's a man—you don't want to go easy on a man. Trust me. Don't ever let a man know how much you care, 'cause he'll just take advantage."

Dionne laughed as she poured herself another glass of champagne.

"That's exactly how I feel sometimes. Like with Mike, all he talks about now is commitment and devotion and all those things. But when I used to talk about those things, he couldn't see it. He couldn't understand it."

Campbell was pleased to hear that Dionne had found faults with Mike. There was hope for him yet.

"So why are you with him?" he asked.

Dionne took another sip from her glass.

"I guess because we've been through many good times as well as some rough ones." She laughed, a touch of irony in her voice. "So what about you? Is there a Mrs Clarke?"

"Not yet," Campbell grinned. "But I'm open to all offers."

"How about kids?"

"Hey, hold on. If I had kids I'd have a woman."

"Not necessarily."

"Yes necessarily. I'm not one of those men who's only out

for one thing," he assured her. "Don't mistake me for a roughneck."

Dionne grinned wickedly. "Pity," she said, emptying the last drop of champagne into her glass. "So what kind of women do you go for?"

"I like a woman who knows what her man needs. I'm a very demanding kinda guy and the type of woman I like appreciates that and knows how to make love."

"When you say, 'make love', don't you mean 'screw'? Aren't you confusing the two things? Women want to make love, men just want a quickie. Making love takes longer than having sex, you know."

"Do I detect a 'men are dogs' tone in your voice?"

"Maybe you do."

They engaged in this friendly 'battle of the sexes' banter for a while longer. As they talked, Campbell slipped his hand so gently in hers that she barely noticed. It felt so good to just touch her, that he lost himself in the wildest fantasies about what could be between himself and Dionne. His heart beat with triple excitement as he imagined kissing her, first gently and then with more passion until the kiss became a caress. He could almost see himself lifting her dress up over her head and caressing her breasts and squeezing her behind. And his sexual anticipation went soaring when he pictured himself easing her legs apart and gently teasing, coaxing and exciting her by spreading her lips with his fingers to search out her undying promises.

Snap out of it, Campbell told himself. *You better come out of it.* He knew himself well enough to know that it wouldn't take much for him to act on impulse and make a move now that he would regret later. For every action there's a reaction and Campbell was fully aware that tonight could have unforetold consequences.

"All my life, I've waited for someone like you," Campbell said dreamily. "I can be your lover and I can be your man. All I need is the the opportunity to show you exactly what I'm feeling. If you give me the chance, I'll take you to places you've never been to before. If you let me, I'll take you to the very edge of your desires. Be good to me, Dionne and I'll be good to you."

But Dionne hadn't heard any of it. All that champagne had taken it's toll and she was now snoozing gently on the bed sofa. Campbell looked at her admiringly. She looked like a sleeping princess. Campbell leant across and gave her a sloppy kiss on her forehead. Dionne's sleepy eyes blinked open. She looked up at his smiling face.

"How long have I been asleep?" she asked.

"Only a minute or two," Campbell replied.

"I am sooooo tired. I really should go home."

"You can stay here the night if you want to."

Dionne smiled. "That's sweet of you," she said, "but you know how it is, I've got a big comfy bed waiting for me at home."

Campbell nodded. "I'll drive you home."

All the way down to the car, Campbell was thinking about how he was going to play it cool with Dionne. He felt that he had a chance with her. He wasn't going to rush things, but he needed to see her once more to convince her that he, and not Mike, was Mr Right.

It didn't take long to get to Hampstead. As Dionne climbed out of the Jag, Campbell told her he had enjoyed the evening so much that he would like to invite her to dinner. "I'll cook for you. I'm a wicked chef."

Dionne had a better idea. "It's my turn to treat you. Look, why don't you come around to my place tomorrow evening. Around seven. I'd like to cook you dinner.

Campbell grinned. "It's a deal," he said, before slipping the Jag into gear and pulling away into the night.

86% of black men find female orgasms unpredictable and cannot be sure when, or sometimes why, they happen. 14% believed that this was a trick question, as experience had taught them that women "do not have orgasms."

TWENTY-FOUR SEVEN

"Man, I'm crazy about her. Seriously crazy about her. This time, it's for real."

The news that Campbell was finally checking a woman was welcomed by Trevor when they met up in the sauna. And even though he took the notion of being in love with the pinch of salt of a cynic, Trevor was prepared to accept it and congratulate his friend for it. He didn't care what Campbell called his feelings, as long as he was now checking woman. It had been long overdue.

"So that's where you've been hiding yourself?" Trevor grinned. "Here I am trying to hook you up with some of the craziest women out there and behind my back you're checking some honey anyway. Well, 'nuff respect, Clarkey."

The sauna was almost empty. Apparently, it had been that way for most of the day. Apart from Trevor and Campbell and a couple of the old-timers, there was no one there. This was the first time in nearly two years that the Black Men United massive had been absent from one of their sessions in the sauna.

"So what's she like?"

Campbell hesitated at first, unsure of exactly what to say. "She's tall, intelligent, fun to be with. She laughs a lot, talks a lot. She can be charming and witty and she can tease and be infuriating and the life of the party. You can never say you really know her. Just when you think you have her down to a science, she reveals a side you never expected.

There's something refreshing about her personality and when she enters a room full of people, everyone knows that she is there. She knows how to make an impact."

"But what does she look like?" Trevor asked eagerly. "Is she fit? Is she criss?"

"I haven't really thought about that."

"Don't gimme that, man. You haven't thought? Okay, let me put it like this then, is she ugly?"

"No, she's not ugly."

"You see what I'm saying, you don't need to think about it, because those things are obvious. That's the first thing you notice. All you've got to do is take one look at her."

"Well in that case, okay, she's attractive. But what do you expect me to say? Of course I think she's the most beautiful girl in the world. She is beautiful."

"That's all I'm asking. And she gives you what you need on the physical side? You get your banana peeled yet?"

Campbell should have guessed that that was what Trevor was thinking about. Hadn't he always? Whenever he dated women, the two things Trevor wanted to know were the two things men always want to know about their friends' new girlfriends: How good looking is she? How does she perform in the sack? And normally he would have been quick to recount the details of a wicked night of bump and grind. But with Dionne it was different and the fact that they hadn't yet slept together was only part of the reason. This woman was special and he didn't feel good about discussing their supposed intimacies. Sure, he could say they'd had sex. In fact he knew what Trevor would say if he told the truth—"You can't love a woman until you've been to bed with her"—and he didn't want to have to argue a position that he knew he couldn't defend.

He did love her, even though he couldn't explain why. He who feels it knows it and he could feel the adrenaline race through his body and rush to his head. He could feel his stomach tighten in knots and he could get lost in thoughts of the future—a future where she featured large in every frame. A future where they lived together, loved together and had children together. A future where they grew old and lived the rest of their lives together with tenderness and sensitivity. He had fantasized about her so much—not only in bed, but in the bath, in the car, on the phone—that he was ready and willing to fall in love quickly, totally and permanently. He was prepared to hug her even when she didn't need a hug, and to be gentle with her. He would compliment her frequently and encourage her and challenge her. He would bite his tongue before he ever said anything that might put her down. He would remember her birthday and they would celebrate their anniversary at the same expensive restaurant every year. Above all he would make her happy. These were the things he wanted to say to her when they met up tonight; that if he was the man she chose for life, he would consider himself the luckiest man in the world. And he was going to say it, he would shout his love for her from the top of Telecom Tower.

"She's great in bed," Campbell lied, hoping that that would be enough. It was only a partial lie, because even though they hadn't actually slept together, in the virtual reality of his most vivid thoughts, that was how he had imagined her, peeling away his resistance, gently and seductively, layer by layer as his temperature slowly rose, titillating all his senses by fondling him to get him in the proper mood, while Al Green sang softly in the background. That was his idea of good sex and once he started fantasizing about her, Campbell found it difficult to get his mind on anything else.

Dionne was a woman who could turn him on with a smile, light his fire with a gentle and tender touch, have him on a leash, yet make him adore being led around. The thought of spending just one night with her was all that was needed to send him into a state of complete and ecstatic oblivion. How many times had he agonised from excitement? Broken out in anticipation? Squirmed from longing at the very thought of her caress? He was hopelessly in love. And happy.

"Okay, she's good in bed, but what's her slam *really* like? Give me the details…"

"Real explosive sex. When she is in the mood, she is insatiable. And she doesn't just lie there either, but gives the wickedest slam. In every position and at any time any place, anywhere. As long as it's different, she'll try it out. Sex in the shower is one of her favourites. Whenever she needs to take a trip down in that love zone, she simply calls me up and tells me not to move a muscle, that she's coming over and by the time she gets to my place, she's so hot. And she knows how to talk dirty during sex and she's got the sweetest sounds of love. Man, if you heard her moaning gently, softly, passionately, you would tear your hair out. You see sex isn't just sex with her, it becomes the ultimate trip, a cosmic experience. And when we make love she insists on having the lights on, because she doesn't want to miss anything and she's got well-placed mirrors in her bedroom, because she likes to see what's going on. When it comes to sex, she don't ramp."

"Stop there…stop there!" Trevor pleaded, feeling horny himself from hearing his friend's graphic account. If Campbell's intention was to put his friend's mind at ease, he had succeeded. Trevor was pleased for him and even said that he could sense the difference that love had made. All Campbell needed was some good sex to straighten himself out and as long as he was getting it, Trevor was happy for him.

Campbell was in a hurry and it was closing time anyway, so after just a quick session in the sauna, he dipped out, showered and got himself ready.

"I wonder what happened to everybody else?" he said, as they were getting dressed in the changing rooms.

Trevor was wondering the same thing. The sauna seemed eerie without the normal rush of black men. "Benji!" he called out to one of the old-timers. "You know what happened to everyone else?"

"Dem gone ah Brixton, the whole ah de massive fe de demonstration."

"Demonstration? What demonstration?"

"You nevah hear 'bout Fat Freddy?"

Both Campbell and Trevor shook their heads.

"You nevah hear 'bout him?! Police lick off him inna the head las' night an' kill him dead."

"Wha'!!!?"

"Yeah, down ah Brixton. Dem say he was resisting arrest."

Neither Campbell nor Trevor could believe their ears. It was like a bad dream. Fat Freddy, dead? That was impossible. Campbell started breathing hard and heavy, his heart pounding, his head swimming. He turned helplessly to Trevor and noticed a tear in his friend's eye. Neither of them knew what to say.

"You sure ah Fat Freddy?"

"Definitely. Ah him one name Frederick Broderick, ain't it?"

Trevor nodded, remembering hearing Fat Freddy's full name once. But could it really be true? It was unbelievable. They listened in mournful silence as Benji told them the story. Apparently Fat Freddy had gone to Brixton the night before to check his baby mother who lived on Railton Road. By all accounts he left her house at about 11.30pm in order to catch the last tube back up to north London. But he had only walked a few yards when a police van suddenly drove onto the pavement in front of him and a number of heavily armed officers jumped out and demanded to know where he was going, where he had been and wanted to search his pockets. Fat Freddy wasn't in the mood for any slackness and told them in no uncertain terms that he wasn't going to explain shit to them. What happened next was unclear, but an eyewitness claimed that Freddy seemed to push one of the officers aside and, seeing this, the other officers pulled out their newly issued American-style batons and beat Freddy unconscious, before dragging him into the back of the van.

He was pronounced dead on arrival at Kings College Hospital an hour later, but the police did not announce his death until that morning, when they released a statement saying that Fat Freddy had died of a heart attack from being so overweight. Everybody who knew that he went to the pool for a swim, gym workout and sauna at least two or three times a week knew that it couldn't be true. He might have been fat, but he was healthy. As each of the sauna users had trickled in during the day, they were told the tragic news. By midday, the initial sorrow of hearing of the death of a brother had turned to anger and everybody was up for going down to Brixton police station to demand the arrest of the officers concerned for murder and there had been calls on all the pirate stations for people to come out in strength and support the demonstration.

"If me was a coupla years younger I woulda been down there meself," Benji said.

Campbell stood shaking his head throughout the old-timer's account of the events. Fat Freddy dead? How could he be? He had seen him just two days before joking and laughing and arguing with everybody as usual, you couldn't keep his mouth shut. How could he be dead?

Trevor was also speechless, a thousand things going through his mind, many of them not too pleasant. He wanted revenge. He wanted someone to pay for the death of his friend. What did Fat Freddy ever do to anyone? He didn't deserve to die. Whatever went down between him and the policemen, he didn't deserve to die.

Campbell and Trevor continued to get dressed in silence. It seemed to take forever to slip on a pair of trousers, a shirt and a jacket. They both knew what they had to do, they didn't need to talk about it. They bid Benji a solemn adieu and made their way out.

By the time they got to Brixton, a sizeable crowd had gathered outside the police station in front of which a line of police officers in riot gear stood, ready to beat down any insurrection. The demonstrators were noisy and angry. They weren't going to be contained this time. Fat Freddy was the second black youth to have died in police custody in six months and this time people weren't going to be pacified with talk of an 'official inquiry'—"How the hell are you going to get the police to investigate the police?" One angry black student yelled at the suggestion by a top ranking officer on the steps of the station.

Campbell and Trevor soon found their friends—Sweetbwoy, Ruffy and Tuffy, Bucky, Mikey. Even Mark, the barrister, had left the court room to come and demonstrate. Now, standing there on Brixton Road in front of the station, the fifty-strong group of men did something they had never done before. They embraced each other. The sight of so many black men with tears in their eyes, hugging each other because they needed a hug, may have seemed unusual at any other time. But just now, with the sound of an angry militant demanding "Justice!" through a megaphone, it didn't seem strange. One or two of them even breaking down and sobbing as memories of Fat Freddy crossed their minds. They all knew what they had to do and they were going to do it. Somewhere, among the gathered friends of Fat Freddy from the sauna, a rock was catapulted into the air and hurtled in an upward arc towards the police station building. The shatter of the plate glass window on the second floor window of the station was like a catalyst for what happened next.

The flames and broken glass were a physical reminder of the frustration Campbell had felt since childhood while out on the streets looking for a brighter day. It may take 100 years for the police to understand this, but as far as most people were concerned, the riot wasn't just about Fat Freddy. It went deeper than that and had been brewing for years.

In the middle of it all, Campbell remembered where he was supposed to be and an image of Dionne formed in his mind. She had to understand that he wouldn't let her down unless it was of vital importance. Freddy's death had to be dealt with and as much as he wanted to see her there was just no way he could or would leave.

Black leaders were crying out that "we need to come together and pray for peace and hope." But the youths needed something more than hope. They needed to teach the police to respect young black men and women, because until then their lives were all in jeopardy. They had petitioned and marched for years and still the government ignored them. So finally it was time to pump up their fists. That night, they reminded the whole country that black men united could give the police a good hiding if necessary. But as always, the police had an ace up their sleeve and that night Campbell and Trevor had to spend the night in jail and were up before the magistrates the next morning.

__BOOK II__

DIONNE'S STORY

I read an article in Cosmo recently about black women who run after their men. Excuse me, but no. I don't run after any man. That's not my style, girl. I don't see the point of it. For one thing men can run faster...and that can leave a girl looking like she's got 'F-O-O-L' written across her forehead. And for another thing, the harder the chase, the bigger the disappointment. And believe me, there's always a disappointment.

One of the advantages of having money is that you don't have to go looking for a man, men flock to you. It's also one of the disadvantages, because you end up searching for the dollar signs in every man's eyes—particularly those who say, "I love you." They think you're going to be so overjoyed because they've said those three little words, that you'll use your money to take them for a ride down 'Cherry Tree Lane'. One or two will even remind you that "black men are in such short supply that you better take me whilst you've still got the chance." Well girl, I'm a rich black woman, and as every rich black woman knows, we are in short supply too.

A man without funds is definitely not my style. If he looks good, smells good, feels good and knows what to do with his sweetness, I might date him. Once, twice, or maybe more, but I wouldn't get serious. A rich man and a poor woman, yes, maybe, but the other way round is asking for trouble. I tried it just once and it didn't work, despite getting more sweetness than I could handle. That short experience of wasting time with a man who wasted time taught me that the old macho male ego always rears

114

its ugly head when a man has to live in his woman's place, drive her car and be taken out to eat at expensive restaurants on her credit card. The thanks I got for wanting to share everything I had with him came in the shape of a hard slap across the face, when I decided to surprise him by booking a well-needed holiday for the two of us to Egypt. Then he had the nerve to say, "You had that coming to you, baby, you've been asking for that a long time." Asking for it? How was I asking for it? Apparently, because I wouldn't stop trying to cut off his balls the same way the white man was doing to him every day. I asked for it, because I thought I was so clever with all my fancy talk and big money. I asked for it because I assumed he wanted to go to Egypt when he would have rather gone to Jamaica. I asked for it, because he didn't have a job and didn't have a hope of finding anything with a salary that wouldn't look like chump change compared to the money I had. I asked for it because the only way he could see enough money to match me was by hitting the jackpot on the lottery and, despite maximum effort, luck was against him. I asked for it for all my buppy friends with all their fancy talk, who tried to make him look stupid every time they came round. And I asked for it because...just because..."Because you're a woman...it's just a woman thing, so take it like a woman—bitch! Besides, black men are under a lot of pressure, we've got good reason to explode."

That was the first and last time anyone ever treated me like that. When he later made a weak attempt to apologise by trying to tell me that black men learned to treat women like shit from the white man's example, I was like, "Put down the comics please and learn some real history."

As usual, the next afternoon he went to spend some more of my money down at the bookies. The moment he was out of the door, I called up the removal firm I had contacted that morning and they sent the team round they had had on standby. In little more than an hour, they had removed all my property from the flat. All I had to do was drive over to the letting agency and hand in the keys. I handed them my notice on the Notting Hill flat and signed a cheque for the next month's rent. I couldn't take any chances, my name was on the lease.

When you've been through something like that, you don't care how much people tell you to look at his heart and not at his wallet, you just want to avoid the same thing happening again. Now the eligible black men I meet, call them buppies or whatever, they would never have behaved like that. I'm not saying they're all perfect, because they're not, but they've got theirs and don't feel humiliated by what I've got. As for slapping me down, most of the men I know are too aware of the criminal implications of assault to even consider it. A rich black man might not be able to give me the same amount of sweet loving, the same amount of stamina and the same amount of satisfaction as my roughneck lover gave me, but all the sweetness in the world couldn't make up for that slap. Real men don't use and abuse their women.

It always seems to start off as a friendship...

A roll in the hay or a one-night stand is not my style either. So Mike and I became lovers, nothing more, just lovers, and even so I always choose my lovers carefully. The bitter taste of the violence at the end of my last relationship had soured my appetite and I wasn't interested in anything more. I was no longer bothered about whether I would ever experience true love. I just wanted to be able to breathe again and get on with my life. All I needed from Mike was sex and a little tenderness. I was simply going to enjoy it while it lasted and then move on. But that wasn't enough for him and he started confusing sex with love and whispering words of eternal commitment to me every time we were together. Well, I wasn't going to make it easy for him.

At first I ignored him, while thinking, "you want to be with me for the rest of your life...yeah right!" But Mike tried everything to turn me round, and what followed was an onslaught of passion from his side. I didn't know what had hit me. There was a bunch of flowers on my doorstep when I got up in the morning and a trio of Spanish musicians outside the house serenading me every *evening.*

After a week of that I had to admit that I was intrigued. Everywhere I turned I was drowning in verse upon verse of his painful poetry, yet I couldn't stop reading it. It didn't just arrive in the mailbag either, but reams of the stuff would spew out of the fax machine and the answering machine was full with the spoken version.

It should have made me angry, but hearing his self-conscious voice trying to sound romantic, I laughed. Starting a relationship means continuing it, then going all the way. Up to now I had only regarded Mike as an occasional partner and before I could take his declarations seriously I needed a basis on which to test him other than his performance in bed. Because it was one thing if he couldn't provide all the physical stimulation I needed—I've got my head and I've got my fantasies and if necessary I don't need nobody else, I can do it all by myself—but if he couldn't provide me with mental stimulation, forget it!

Mike invited me to a private weekend at the Grand Hotel in Brighton where he had booked the most expensive suite in which he arranged for music, chilled champagne, silk robes...and which had a beautiful bath equipped with a variety of scented soaps and oils. We didn't leave the suite once, the entire weekend. All we did was drink champagne, have sex in the shower and exchange fantasies while Mike performed the most sensuous hot massage, which had every inch of my body tingling, and went to great pains to prove that he had a penetrating mind by talking of existentialism, Sartre and Camus, and the nineties as the decade of the unfulfilled orgasm. I had to admit that I was intrigued. Then he mentioned marriage and before I knew it, he had proposed.

For me, love is all or nothing (both giving and receiving), but I know the ways of the world and the shortcomings of most men too well to expect more than I can see and hold in my hand. However, falling in love is one of the sweetest things and when something that nice happens, you start to dream the mystical dream that maybe, just maybe, you've found someone who means it when they say, "For the rest of my life I only ever want to make love to you…" It sounded so sincere when Mike said it, that I took time out to consider the proposal before answering.

I told him that I wanted adventure and didn't consider myself housewife material and he said that he wasn't looking for one anyway. And I told him all the other things I'd expect from a husband. Above all else I wanted devotion and he promised that I would get nothing less. To prove his point he pampered me some more and by the end of that weekend I was convinced that I was deeply in love and that Mike Phillips was the man I wanted to marry. I even had to say 'no' to another suitor in order to say 'yes' to Mike.

Why can't love be like a fairy tale? Why has there always got to be disappointment?

I mean, I love being in love. When I'm in love I'm happy and on a natural high. For probably the first time in my life, I had met a man who understood my feelings and desires. He was a steady, reliable lover who didn't have a deep penetration or an elaborate sexual technique, yet the orgasms I achieved with him were among the most intense I'd ever had, for what he lacked in 'expertise' he made up for with heavy foreplay, touching me like I'd never been touched before and learning the trick of making me weak with the slightest caress of my breasts.

It was all lovey dovey until an unexpected phone call one afternoon a year later (he couldn't even face me). His voice sounded like he was in a panic, stammering and jabbering and shifting and avoiding. He said he didn't know how to say what he had to say. As if by magic, Mike, who always knew just the right words to whisper in my ear, had suddenly found himself dumbstruck. I finally managed to prise it out of him though…he was sorry, he didn't mean it to be like this, but he wasn't sure about things any longer. He simply regretted having brought up the subject of marriage in the first place.

I was stunned…

Mike had become my doctor, my lawyer, my teacher, my father, my brother, as well as my lover. I had shared my darkest secrets with him. I had told him my fantasies and what I liked done to me and I had listened patiently to his sexual needs as well. He had given me the emotional support to embrace my weaknesses and I had lifted his spirits sky high and made him feel like the most special person walking the earth. He was always saying how lucky he considered himself after he proposed to me and I said, 'yes'. We had even talked of a home and I had begun to dream of a happy married life and 2.4 children…

Yet, with all that behind us he expected to slide out of our relationship with a "I hope you understand…"

I don't get angry too often, but when he said that I was raging. I was already boiling from feeling deceived by him, he didn't have to insult my intelligence also. It was just as well he was telling me everything down a phone line because when I get this angry, I have to punch someone or throw something.

And with that phone call, all the romance and sensuality of our relationship vanished.

I should have trusted my instincts from the start and just stuck to the sex. If I had relied on my snap judgment, I wouldn't have had the wool pulled over my eyes and I wouldn't have got hurt.

And even though it's been nearly a month, it's still painful. Maybe the pain is part of being a woman in our culture. Because I don't know a single woman who hasn't been hurt like that.

In future I'll make my own luck and my own misery. I'm a positive woman. If I find a man I want to settle down with, someone who I'll move mountains for then fine. If not, I'll make it on my own.

As for Mike, he's still crawling around somewhere under my skin.

7% of the black men currently married are cheating on their wives, either on a regular (3%) or an irregular (4%) basis. 27% of the remainder admitted that they would if they knew they could get away with it, while a further 14% said that the Bobbit episode had cured them of 'infidelititis'.

PIECES OF A MAN

To say that Dionne had been vexed with Campbell for not showing up, when they were supposed to have dinner, was an understatement. She had laid on a really special meal for him which had taken her over three hours to prepare and she had even eased herself in the mood with a little Barry White on the CD player.

They had left the arrangement pretty loose.

"Just come round after eight but before nine," she had said. And Campbell replied that he couldn't wait.

But he didn't show up.

She sat waiting for him, lighting one cigarette after another, flicking from one TV channel to another with the remote control, and trying to tell herself that he had just been held up and that he would call and say as much. But there wasn't even so much as a message on the answering machine. So much for the roughneck lovers. She wasn't going to make the mistake of crossing the class divide again. But Campbell had seemed so different.

Mike, however, did call. He called several times, but Dionne didn't feel like answering. She screened every call and when she heard his voice remained seated in her chair and listened.

"Hi baby, it's me, Mike. Gimme a call. It's important."

"Dee honey, I need to speak to you, A.S.A.P. You got my

121

number. Please, give me a call."

"Okay Dionne, you're obviously not picking up the phone, so I'll tell you why I'm phoning. Baby, you've been on my mind. All night, all day. I can't live without you, baby. I know that now. I want to make you my queen, to honour, love and respect. I want to give you devotion."

Finally around ten o'clock in the evening, Dionne jumped to the phone and picked it up. The first thing he did was say that he would never give her reason to doubt his love again. Then he proceeded to spend more than an hour sweet-talking her.

"I got you a present," he said.

"If it's a birthday present, you're too late."

"It's just a present."

"Oh."

"You don't sound too pleased," he said.

"I'm just tired." She didn't want to go into the fact that she had been stood up and made a fool of earlier in the evening.

"Maybe I can come by and wake you up a little."

Dionne paused long enough to consider the suggestion.

"Yes, why not. Mummy's gone away for the night and I'm in the mood for a long, slow back rub."

Any man would be crazy not to fall over themselves when a woman put it like that. Mike almost tripped over his feet, but he got to Dionne's within twenty minutes. To his surprise, she had laid on a candlelit meal for him. He waited while she selected a Marvin Gaye album from the collection, then they sat down for their midnight meal while Marvin urged them both to get it on.

The meal seemed to go on for hours, during which time they talked about everything under the sun and teased each other about their intimate fantasies.

Later they pulled out some bean bags and sat on the floor cross-legged to watch some videos of old black and white films on the wide-screen television, whispering sweet nothings in each other's ears. He knew the things she liked to hear, secrets that he wouldn't tell anybody else. It was just like the early days with Mike and any thoughts she may have had about Campbell were slowly being eased away.

"So where's this present you've got for me?" Dionne suddenly remembered.

Mike beamed a huge smile, went to his jacket in the hallway and returned with an envelope which he handed over to her. Dionne opened it expectantly. Inside were two airline tickets. London to Acapulco.

"Before you say anything," Mike interjected, "let me say what I've got to say."

He went down on one knee and held Dionne's hand timidly.

"Dionne Owen, I know I've made my mistakes and I've said things that hurt you, I can't do anything about that but I can make things perfect between us if you give me the chance, this second chance, to ask you to marry me. Because in all of the time since I've known you, my love for you has grown and grown. I'm not interested in any other woman. I don't ever want any other woman in my life. You see, nothing has changed. I love you more today than yesterday and when tomorrow comes around I'll love you even more. You are the woman I want to be with every day from morning until the sun goes down, for the rest of my life. You are the woman I want to build a home with and have children with. You don't know what you've done to me. I never used to care much for moonlit nights or candlelit dinners, until you showed me the light. Baby, if you want someone that understands you…that needs your love all the time, someone to be with when you're up and someone to be with when you're down, then just say you'll marry me and I'll be right here for you. All you have to do is say the words and everything will work out fine."

Sometimes you get what you want and you lose what you had. Dionne had mixed feelings about Mike's second proposal. But when a man gets down on one knee and offers you the world, love leads you to the altar.

"What about the way you love me?" she asked, probing and analysing. "Isn't your love going to wane again? It has once before. How can I be sure you're not going to become unsure once more? It's too easy for you to say you love me and you want to be with me for the rest of your life, but marriage has built-in conditions, strings attached."

"Dionne baby, you don't ever have to worry about that because I now know what I should have known all along. I know the meaning of those three little words: love, honour and obey."

Mike remained like that, until the ache in his knee was too much, urging Dionne that they should get married and soon. He reminded her of all the good times they had had together and of all the wonderful things that he now wanted to do for her. There's only so much of that a girl can take before she starts believing the hype. *But maybe it isn't hype.* Dionne had her dreams and dreams *can* sometimes come true.

The next day, they were on the flight to Acapulco.

Getting married seemed so easy. Acapulco was a city made for lovers and they were able to arrange a quickie wedding.

When they returned to London from their two-week honeymoon, Valerie Owen was deeply upset that her daughter had married without her knowledge. The only way around her disappointment was to throw a belated reception at her home for the bride and groom. It was an impromptu affair for close friends and relatives, hardly the ball at the Savoy that she had always dreamed that she would one day hold for her only daughter on her wedding day.

Her old friend Stella also felt aggrieved that Dionne had married in secret. She had always envisaged being there to support Dionne on the happiest day of her life. And the girl had gone off and tied the knot without even a hint to her.

"So what do you think?"

Stella sat back in her chair at Mezzo's and weighed up the question. What could she say? It was too late for her opinion. Dionne was already married. She turned her attention back to her friend who was waiting eagerly for her approval. Best friend or not, Dionne looked too happy for her to spoil it by telling her what she really thought. She had never been too impressed with Mike Phillips, but that didn't deter her friend from seeing him for more than a year and it hadn't stopped her from becoming his wife. To Stella, Mike was just...boring! BORING. Why did he always have to talk about himself and about how wonderful he was and how much money he was making, and the biggest deals he had concluded that day and how much money he was going to be making? Why did he fantasize so much about fame and success and what he was going to do when he became famous and even more successful? You only had to spend a few minutes with Mike Phillips to realise how shallow he was, yet Dionne had believed the hype. And there was something else about him that Stella didn't like. Though he was of Caribbean origin, Mike sounded white and looked white in all his mannerisms, his laughter his jokes—everything. He seemed to be able to imitate white people better than most white people—the way they walk, dress and their vocabulary. It wasn't a class thing, because you could still be black and middle class. Mike on the other hand, apart from his skin colour, seemed to have lost all his blackness. In fact, he seemed to take pride in this and

125

enjoyed going out of his way to criticise "the average black man" for not working hard enough to establish himself in this country like the Asians have done. Stella's silent sigh came from deep within. Mike just wasn't the right man for Dionne.

"Well?" Dionne asked eagerly, expectantly.

Stella searched frantically for words. But she knew her friend well enough to guess that Dionne didn't want to hear what she really thought. Despite herself Stella beamed a broad smile. "Congratulations!"

That was what Dionne wanted to hear! She jumped to her feet with a shriek, which caused some of the upmarket clientele in Mezzo's to turn a disapproving eye in their direction. But the two girlfriends had already abandoned polite restaurant decorum in favour of youthful exuberance and were locked in a tight, joyful embrace.

"Oh, I knew you'd be happy for me," Dionne said excitedly, once they eventually sat down at the discreet request of the elegantly dressed waiter. He collected the dishes from their table in what seemed like one swift movement. "Isn't Mike just..." she couldn't find the words to express what she wanted to say and finally concluded the point with a wave of her hand.

Stella smiled at her friend and they clinked champagne glasses in a toast to all that Mike Phillips was and all that he was to become in marriage with Dionne.

Then Dionne filled Stella in on the details of how she and Mike had married in the 'Chapel of Love'.

"That's what it was called, but it wasn't much more than a wooden shack on a little country lane just outside Acapulco. But girl, it was like magic. Believe me. Wait until you see the photographs."

"Look, D," Stella began cautiously, she was treading on delicate ground here with a friend who she knew could easily lose her temper over the smallest wrong comment.

Dionne wouldn't hesitate to leave the table in a huff and walk out of the restaurant, slamming the door behind her. But Stella had to find out why Dionne had married a man who had nothing to do with her romantic ideal. Why was she with a one-dimensional man?

"Stella girl, this is the man of my dreams. I know I've made the right decision."

That made Stella even less convinced. No way was Mike the man of Dionne's dreams. They had been best friends since secondary school and she knew everything about Dionne. She had known the different men of Dionne's dreams since they were old enough to start dreaming about men. Yes, Robert De Niro had once been the man of her dreams. And so had Prince, Rick James, Eddie Murphy, Denzel Washington. Lately she had been dreaming of Wesley Snipes and Laurence Fishburne. Those guys *never* looked like accountants and those guys knew how to really charm a woman, instead of talking about themselves all the time. While Mike was taken up with planning his strategy for making more and more money, he had never seemed to realise that Dionne was a woman who clung on to beautiful romantic fantasies. Fantasies about making love while bathing in perfumed water, and being showered with love and affection as she walks on a beach under a full moon, wading barefoot in the evening grass, wrapped in a soft, fluffy blanket with sweet whispered promises of the most exquisite and forbidden sex… Dionne fantasized not just of physical contact, but more importantly of gentleness, ebbing and flowing into an ocean of desire. The man who could help turn those fantasies into realities was the man of Dionne's dreams. And, sorry, but Mike wasn't that man.

And who was he trying to impress, with his grandiose claims of how he singlehandedly dragged his company out of the recession, by making some "big deals"? The more Mike talked about money, the more Stella realised that this was a man who wasn't used to it. She had had money most of her life and was accustomed to wealth. In fact, she found it rather vulgar to talk about it. Instead of boasting about it, she was rather reluctant to tell people that her father was a millionaire—several times over. And only her closest friends knew that she was Stella De Souza as in *the* De Souzas! The family who had made a fortune marketing cosmetics for black women and whose products had made their way onto the shelves of every high street supermarket. When you were an heir to that sort of money you didn't have to keep saying it.

Their families had moved to Hampstead at about the same time in the early eighties. It was coincidence that the two girls should have attended the same school, also, but when their parents decided to send their daughters to a private day school, they both chose St Philomena's at the top of Highgate Hill. Dionne and Stella quickly became close friends and spent not only their time at school together, but also a lot of their time outside school as well.

In those days it was usually somewhere like a museum or an art gallery. Nowadays, they were more likely to be seen at clubs or parties. As neither of them had to work for a living, they could rave all night long if they wanted to. They had shared a lot of laughs in all this time and a lot of heartaches as well. Now in their mid-twenties, they were still as loyal to each other as they had ever been and were willing to put up with each others' occasional tantrums to remain good friends.

When it came to men, there wasn't anything they didn't tell each other. But lately the subject of love had become a touchy one with Dionne. It was alright for Stella to say you don't want to rush into things. She had her man already. She was going to marry Lee the moment he came back from his studies in California. He was adorable. A real preppy black man with youthful looks and a smile that could make your heart melt. What's more Lee was a lot of fun to be around. Everything about him was pretty cool, the way he dressed, the things he had to say. And he had a big laugh which always endeared him to people he had only just met for the first time.

"I decided to marry Mike because I'm tired of all the phony guys I keep meeting," Dionne continued. "You know the ones who are quick to say, 'I know that you're rich and that's why I'm gonna do whatever it takes to be with you'. And even when you're being a bitch, they'll accept it because you're a rich bitch. I'm not sayin' that's the way it is across the board. Sometimes you meet guys with a little bit more flavour than that. Like Mike. He's nice. He's funny. He loves me for the laughs we share and the tears we spare. And…you know…I fell for him…I never felt like this before, girl. When we were in Acapulco I was writing poems every day. Can you imagine? Me writing poetry! Everything seemed so beautiful I had to put pen to paper, girl. And when night-time came and we made love I felt like singing him a love song in bed. And when I rocked him softly to sleep, I started thinking the craziest things…"

Stella simply listened. Could love really have this effect on someone? Dionne had always been easily swayed and impressed at the start of a relationship, but if anyone had said that she would disappear for two weeks and come back with a wedding ring on her finger and a head full of soppy romantic ideas, Stella would have said 'no way'.

Stella thought about her own situation. She had made a decision to wait for Lee, but was well aware that anything could happen in the time it took to complete a PhD. Who knows? Lee might find some other woman while he was at college in the States. There were enough beautiful women in California to distract his mind while he was studying. Both she and Dionne knew what it was to stand and watch, with a twinge of trepidation, as one by one almost all their friends had ended up married. But Stella was prepared to keep waiting for her share of beautiful sunsets even if things didn't work out right with Lee. She wasn't going to rush into anything.

"I want to be married, but I won't marry for the sake of being married," she had always said. "You have to know someone really well before you commit to them. You have to be soulmates."

Dionne had made some bad mistakes in her time but Mike Phillips could be the worst mistake of all.

Had she forgotten how he had dissed her and said he didn't love her any more? That it was just a matter of falling out of love with someone over a period of time? That Dionne wasn't the woman he wanted to spend the rest of his life with? The man had even said that maybe he could grow to love her again—eventually—maybe in a few years...he would think about it. But right now he just didn't love her any more and had agonised for three nights before building up the courage to let her know. How could Dionne have forgotten all of that?

Stella shook her head, visibly confused. She glanced over at Dionne who was gazing dreamily at her wedding ring. She really did look 'in love' and right then Stella knew one thing for certain. Love sure was blind.

Dionne moved into Mike's bachelor pad in Knightsbridge on her return from Acapulco. But it was only a temporary arrangement. For a woman who was used to living in a Hampstead villa, the one bedroom apartment seemed tiny. But when you're in love, small things like that don't matter, well not for too long.

After nearly two months of married life, Dionne still seemed to be a girl about town and carried on doing all the things she had been doing before—seeing Stella, going out shopping and partying. She had told Mike from the beginning that she didn't want to become a housewife. She didn't like cooking and wouldn't cook. Mike could learn if he wanted to, but she wouldn't do it willingly. She didn't like washing dishes, so they needed to get a dishwasher and she didn't want to be tied down to a life of routines. If he wasn't really into partying that was fine, she wouldn't distress him, she would go without him. He had to respect that she was never going to just stay in and spend her days cooking and cleaning, a domestic life was not for her.

Mike said that he was happy as long as she was happy, but every now and then he would forget that she wasn't the conventional wife and leave his dirty underwear out for her to wash.

They had only been shopping a couple of hours, and most of that time on South Molton Street, yet they had already spent more money on clothes than a lot of women earn in a month. There were so many 'bargains' in the West End that they found it hard to go from one designer wear shop to another without picking something up. And besides, Dionne was unrelenting. It was her treat. Her way of thanking Stella for the trip to the Alps. She had insisted on getting her friend a whole new outfit with a wide hat to go with it, because Ascot was coming up soon and Dionne knew her friend hadn't bought any new hats this season.

By the time they got to their hair appointments at Frazzles in Soho, they were loaded down with fancy bags and laughing so much they had each forgotten any other worries.

As always, Frazzles was busy and buzzing when they arrived, the five stylists doing their best to accommodate the heavy schedule of bookings, while people sat around chatting, watching and waiting for their turn in front of the mirror. Some of the smiling faces were well-known to the two girlfriends. These regulars were well respected for the way they looked and took their styling seriously in every aspect, from the way they dressed, to the way they walked and talked. Some of the regulars—men and women, Frazzles did both—looked so good in their chic clothes that they were desperately trying to stifle proud smiles because they didn't want to make it look like a big deal. They wanted it to seem like they always dressed like this, even in their sleep.

Angelo smiled when he saw his homegirls. He was the most popular of Frazzles' stylists and numbered a member of the royal family among his illustrious clients, and there were only two black hairdressers in the whole of Britain who could claim that distinction. Of the two, Angelo was the more handsome. Built like a Michelangelo sculpture, his stunning good looks and sharp dress sense had endeared him to the media and he was now the darling of all the women's magazines and several of the men's ones too. He was a man who manufactured his own sunshine and could lighten up the dullest day or any of the many tales of woe which his clients confided in him. Many of his wealthier customers could afford to book appointments just to have Angelo cheer them up. Even confirmed pessimists were forced to smile at his childlike optimism about absolutely everything and anything.

Dionne and Stella were two of his favourite customers. They took care of their hair and generally booked a weekly appointment together to get it touched up. He loved working on them as much as he had done when they first became his clients almost three years ago. More than that, he loved trading gossip with them and had even discovered that they all shared similar tastes in men! Just like Dionne and Stella, Angelo liked his men hot and black!

"You've been out spending on your mummies' credit

cards again dears?" He chided, indicating their shopping bags. "Girlies will be girlies!"

But Angelo was just as keen to see what was in those shopping bags and inspected each article of clothing with the trained eye of a women's couture expert.

He sat his clients down in chairs beside each other and began working on both of them together. Stella and Dionne had similar hair and always insisted on the same haircuts. As their hair grew at pretty much the same rate they generally needed a retoucha t the same time. He was a true master of his work and he could easily give two haircuts at a time.

"So how was the holiday, Miss Owen?" Angelo asked.

"Mmmmmmnnnnnn..." Dionne answered lazily. Angelo was massaging the shampoo so gently with his delicate fingers that she was feeling aroused and dreamy.

"Enough of the 'Miss'," Stella quipped. "Say congratulations Ange, you're talking to the new Mrs Dionne Phillips."

"Congratulations?" Angelo lighted up. "That deserves more than congratulations, that deserves a celebration. Go girl, what's he like...? Carol!" He called to his assistant. "Open up a bottle of champagne love...there's some Bollinger in the fridge." Then turning eagerly back to Dionne. "What's he like? Is he rich? Is he tall? What's he like in bed?"

Dionne laughed off all his questions, but by now everybody else in the salon was interested.

"He's cool. It's the same man I've been dating for over a year now. We just decided to tie the knot. I needed someone to love and someone to love me and he needed someone to love and someone to love him. The main thing is that we're both happy."

Stella confirmed it. "When I've seen them together they've looked so happy."

"If you can get a minute of happiness these days dears, you should take it. Who would have believed it, eh?" Angelo continued. "A month ago...who would have believed it...? Here we were all three of us, asking ourselves where all the good men had gone. And now, imagine, Dionne's married, I'm 'married' and Stella will be married as soon as her sweetheart finishes his studies...didn't I tell you that this was going to be a good year for us girls?"

The champagne had arrived. Angelo declared the toast, "to an end of forever seeking sex partners in a vain search for satisfaction...may we all find satisfaction in the simple pleasures of monogamy—with some good sex as well of course!"

The haircuts were on the house, Angelo insisted, because they were celebrating. Not just the fact that Dionne had got married, but that he had also found Mr Right. After frequent, tragic love affairs and months of feeling lonely, he had found that one perfect mate, an intellectual and emotional counterpart, a knight in shining armour who had come to rescue him from his loneliness. Now at last, Angelo's faith in black men had been revived. There were some good ones out there, you just had to look hard for them. But it was worth the wait, he declared, every minute of it.

"But before I forget my manners, I don't want to steal your steam, DeeDee. You haven't told me what he's like. Oh he must be really special," Angelo gushed.

"Oh, he's nothing special..." Dionne answered coyly.

"Oh, in that case then he must have a really big dick!" Angelo teased. "Well you'll have to bring him round to get his hair done...I can't wait to get my hands on him..."

The things that love could do for you. Mike wanted to come home from work early every night...even though the fellas were calling him up and inviting him to one place or another, he preferred to be at home with his woman and spent as much time as he could with her. As much as Dionne enjoyed his company, she didn't think he should cut himself off from the rest of the world just because he was married and encouraged him to spend more time with his friends. But Mike was so reluctant that she even had to push him out of the flat to go to a rugby international at Twickenham with some of his old public school cronies.

They had been married for just over two months when Dionne realised that her period was late. Even though she knew she was as regular as clockwork, she waited a week before going to the chemist and buying a home test kit. And even though it confirmed her suspicions, she went to her Harley Street doctor for a second opinion.

The first thing Dr Patel asked when he saw her was, "Are you pregnant?" Dionne wasn't expecting that, even though her GP had known her since she was a teenager, when her mother decided to switch to a private health care plan, and could tell—even at this early stage—that there was something different about her, something he had seen in many women before. She was overjoyed.

Mike was over the moon when she told him the news later that evening. He hugged her and kissed her and caressed her stomach. He even talked about his 'son' like the proud father. He popped open a bottle of champagne from the fridge to celebrate. If he had had a cigar in the flat he would have gone for that too.

Dionne reminded Mike that they would have to find somewhere else to live. "We could always move into mummy's house for a while. Until we find something."

Mike said that he didn't think that was a good idea. "I get the feeling that she doesn't like me that much."

"Of course she does," said Dionne abstractedly, "anyway, she would love to have her grandchild around."

Mike maintained that he wouldn't feel comfortable at his mother-in-law's and promised that *he* would sort out a bigger apartment.

Just then his mobile rang. He flipped it open and spoke for a few moments before snapping the phone shut.

"Can you believe it," he said, turning to Dionne, "even when you're at home they don't leave you alone."

He flashed the confident smile of someone who was such a key link in his company that they couldn't do without him.

"Darling, I'm going to have to dash…the market in New York is getting nervous and I need to be there trying to figure out which way it's going to go. It looks like it's going to be a long night because they're five hours behind us of course. Anyway, I'll call you as soon as I can sweetie and maybe we can do something late, late, late…"

Dionne beamed a loving smile at her man.

"Yes of course, darling. You go and take care of business."

She was used to it and waved him goodbye without complaint. After all, now they were married, Mike's business was her business."

One evening a week later, Mike came hòme beaming like a man who had just won the lottery. He had found the perfect place. "Picture a little love nest down where the roses grow, picture yourself lying in a grassy meadow, or on a bed of leaves with a canopy of stars over your head. Imagine just the right environment to make our mutual dreams come true. Now, picture this same little love nest and think what a year can bring—like the patter of tiny feet —and I'm sure you'll agree that this home is ideal."

Mike was so good at building up his wife's expectations that all Dionne wanted to know was where this place was and how soon they could go and view it.

"Well, it's not that easy…you see, the house is in

Horsham."

"Horsham?"

"Yes, you know, in Sussex?"

"Sussex!"

"Yes, I know, I know. But honey, if you see the house, you'll know what I mean. It's a dream home."

If the choice was just hers, Dionne would probably have elected to live her life in the city where she was born and grew up. But she was starting a new phase in her life now. Maybe it was time to let go of the old?

They went down to view the next day. It was a plush eighteenth century farmhouse, decorated in laid-back good taste and full of beautiful appartments. It was set in some six acres of its own land, about three miles outside Horsham. And it really was beautiful. It had three bedrooms on the upper floor, with a bathroom. Downstairs there was a huge kitchen with an old-fashioned woodfire oven, an impressive dining room and a subtly understated, oak-beamed living room with a massive open fireplace. She fell in love with it.

As she wandered around the house, Dionne started imagining what it would be like to live there, especially after she had made a few alterations. She went upstairs again to take another look at the sumptuous bedroom. With its soft lighting, it had an erotic feel to it. She started picturing what it would look like with a few yards of rose-coloured curtains. She could definitely see herself going to bed in it, with some romantic music in the background and Mike bringing up some cocoa and a box of rich liqueurs. It was the perfect backdrop for them to settle in for a night of serious lovemaking or for enjoying tempestuous tumbles together every lazy Sunday morning. It was a house made for great romance and where they could establish a comfortable home together and quietly raise a family and gather possessions.

"We're not that far from London, so you can always go

up to town to see a show or something and we can have lots of dinner parties or get friends down to stay for the weekend. As for your mum, she's only a phone call away. Believe me darling, London isn't everything. There is a whole world out here to explore."

"Can we afford it?" Since marrying she no longer had the reign of her mother's money although she had enough to keep her in the way she was accustomed. Increasingly, she was having to learn to be self-sufficient.

"Baby, don't I always take care of the finances? Don't I always keep the funds flowing?"

He then set about convincing her that even though she had set her heart on working as an assistant for Angus Thompson, there were bound to be lots of other photographers in Horsham who she could work with.

When his wife agreed, Mike looked like the happiest man in the world. His dream was going to be fulfilled. He was married to the woman he loved, he was a successful stockbroker, he was about to become a father for the first time and he was going to buy the house he wanted to live in.

The paperwork was done very quickly. They followed the estate agent back to his office in Horsham and exchanged details. Mike was able to secure a favourable mortgage from the bank he worked for and they were able to exchange contracts just in time to move in before Christmas.

It would take another three months for the novelty of living in the countryside to wear off, and at first Dionne enjoyed it. Just as Mike had said, several of their friends and family came to their weekly dinner parties and often stayed the whole weekend. Dionne's charm was worth coming all the way from London to savour, even for black people who were attached to London like flies to fly paper.

Dionne began to slip comfortably into the role of wife

and expectant mother as though it was what she had always dreamt of. Mike would leave home at 7.45 in the morning, to catch the 8.15 to London with the other commuters. Dionne usually got up at 10am, sometimes later and, after a light breakfast, would occupy herself with either minor DIY around the house or gardening. If it wasn't raining she might even go down to the local stables and book a horse for an hour or two's riding in the nearby woods. In the afternoon, she generally drove into town to shop.

She had traded in the Vitara for a Range Rover in which she liked to explore the West Sussex countryside. Sometimes she drove all the way down to the coast, to Worthing, or Littlehampton. Now that she was this close to the sea, she relished taking the opportunity to get some sea air into her lungs. She had even made the acquaintance of a few of her neighbours who had invited her over for afternoon tea. They were all housewives and keen to hear what the only black couple in the area were really like.

Kathy and Rachel were close friends. Like Dionne, they were housewives whose husbands worked in London. They were conservative with both a small and a big 'C'. But they were also charming, and inexhaustibly enthusiastic. Sometimes the three would drive into town to watch an afternoon matinee and at other times, they would go to the local WI together. The Women's Institute! *Stella wouldn't believe me if I told her.*

After six months of this, however, Dionne began to stay at home more and more. The clinic had confirmed that she was expecting twins and now her stomach was so big that going on afternoon adventures had become too uncomfortable. To make matters worse, most of her friends had trekked all the way down to see them at least once but were reluctant to be parted from their beloved London for a second visit. During this period, the telephone became an extension of Dionne's personality and she spent whole days chatting to her mom, Stella, Kathy or Rachel.

Every now and then she would call Mike at work, but he always felt so uncomfortable about it that she normally resisted the temptation as much as possible. It was just that sometimes she wanted to tell him when one of his unborn children had kicked her. She thought he ought to know. But Mike would always remind her that he had such a high powered job he didn't have that much time to be chatting on the phone. "That's not what they're paying me for." And, as always, Dionne would apologise for ringing before hanging up. Before she got married she would've have gotten angry and hung up on him mid-sentence. But she was different now. Marriage and the prospect of motherhood had drastically changed her.

Still, she was firm in her knowledge that if she lost an argument in the living room, she'd win it back in the bedroom, where she could give her body but control her husband's mind. She had come to the conclusion that Mike would never be able to give her sexual satisfaction. That first time was a fluke, because since then she had never managed an orgasm with him. That didn't matter to her. She was happy to be there for him on those nights when he wasn't totally exhausted when he came home from a hard day at the office. After all, he worked hard and treated her well and besides, she had those long afternoons in the house alone to fantasize about a steamy encounter in the back seat of a limousine with a tall, dark, handsome chauffeur.

It was at the beginning of summer that their twin daughters Imani and Noir arrived. The couple were overjoyed, not only had they been blessed, but they had been blessed twice. The twins' births had taken their marriage beyond the point of no return.

In that first year of marriage, everything was lovey dovey. Dionne did her utmost to be a good wife and mother and Mike relished playing the role of breadwinner. Like a hunter out to gather food for his family, he would only depart on the long journey to work every weekday morning after prolonged hugs and kisses with his wife. In the evenings, when he returned exhausted from work, the first thing he did was to waltz around the living room with Dionne in his arms, while he told her about all the wheeling and dealing he had done during the day and while he listened to what she had been up to and got a progress report on the twins. It was all good, and Dionne believed it would last forever. She was happy.

Mike couldn't do enough for his baby daughters. He made sure that he didn't make any appointments at the weekend in order to be at home as much as possible. He was the proudest father and had the wildest dreams for his children's future. Imani, who was three minutes older than her sister, was going to become the Prime Minister, her father decided. She was a natural leader who already dominated her sister and knew how to get what she wanted from her parents. Noir would probably become a supermodel, Mike predicted, or maybe marry an African prince, as her dimples gave her a slight edge in the beauty stakes and when she smiled, the sun seemed to shine bright.

But having children also brought the first hint of tension in the newlyweds' relationship. As much as he loved his wife and daughters, Mike was not into being woken up in the middle of the night by screaming babies and resisted any urge to go and pick them out of their cot in the nursery to attend to them. That was Dionne's job, he insisted. For one thing, he was out every day of the week working hard, so why should he also have to take care of the babies? And anyway, Imani usually cried in the middle of the night because she wanted food and once she started crying her sister would usually follow. Only one of their parents could feed them, and *he* didn't have breasts.

His tone had taken Dionne by surprise. It was the closest

they had come to having a fight and the ease with which Mike had got vexed troubled her. All she had meant was that he could make a contribution to bringing up the babies.

"You work eight hours a day," she said, "but I work around the clock. It would be difficult enough with one child, but I've got double trouble. If you think it's so easy, we'll swap. I'll go out and work and you can stay home with the twins."

Mike told her that that was hardly an option. She couldn't earn as much money as he was earning and besides, at this age, Imani and Noir needed their mother more than they needed their father.

Dionne let it go. It wasn't worth it. They were both tired and ratty and there was no need to dwell on something so trivial.

She got up, collected the twins from their cot and before long, managed to quieten them down. They weren't hungry, all they needed was a hug.

As soon as she could, after the twins were born and she had found a local nanny to come in three or four times a week and give her a hand with the babies, Dionne made every effort to get back in shape. She enrolled in a gym in town and was constantly trying to improve on what nature had given her. The fact that she had changed her diet helped as well, because she had lost the taste for meat during her pregnancy and the only flesh that passed her mouth was a little fish every now and then.

Sex with her husband felt alright, but nothing more. Nothing to shout about. Mike still didn't know how to light her fire and no longer seemed bothered to learn, for though he was intellectually interested in the idea he was less concerned about the physical reality. And besides, he was often too tired from discharging all his stockbroking responsibilities to have his heart on his sex life.

She seldom saw signs of his previously high sex drive,

except for "Sunday night after the babies have gone to sleep, Dee, but before it gets too late" and she had to satisfy herself with diminished amounts of sweetness, though he still gave her hugs and respect.

And then during a long-distance phone conversation with Stella, who was visiting Lee in California, Dionne began to wonder whether she should talk to her husband.

"You should tell him how you feel, girl," urged Stella once Dionne had filled her in, "I can't believe that the former Miss Dionne Owen is just sitting back and taking the crap."

Now, there is a time to remain silent and a time to speak out. Dionne knew she should have talked to her husband— have a heart to heart, bring everything out in the open. She should have told him in no uncertain terms that she wanted to move back to London, but after all the time and money they had spent on buying the farmhouse she couldn't bring herself to do more than hint at how much sweeter their love could be in the city. Mike didn't seem to get the message however.

He avoided the issue by overwork—leaving for the office earlier and staying there longer. *Is he having an affair?* No, because she had called the office to check and he was there working. Apart from one evening when he didn't come home at all. And when she called the office, the phone just rang and rang and rang. No message, no phone call, nothing. He just didn't show. Not until the next evening, when he simply strolled in as if he had left home that morning as usual, as if there was nothing untoward. She waited for him to say something. But no, they sat down to dinner with Mike talking about the biggest deal of the day and how he was one of the most successful brokers at his bank. Dionne couldn't believe it. She didn't want to bring it up, why should she. It was for him to explain. She didn't want to seem as if she was keeping tabs on him, but how could he come home to his wife without a single word of where he had been the whole night?

They had gone to bed with Mike still droning on about how rich he was going to be, but all she could think about was, 'where were you last night…where were you?' She was thinking so hard, she felt herself becoming sick. She got up and went to the bathroom, just to get away from her husband's interminable monologues.

She couldn't take it any more. She tried to tell him but he pretended not to hear and continued as before. She stared in his face, her mouth shaping the syllables, 'where were you last night'? She shaped them very carefully, but Mike was so enjoying the sound of his own words that even if she had taken a pen and written the question down in a book he would have probably been blind to it. She should have slapped him right there and then. That would have been a message he would have understood clearly. But she didn't, marriage had mellowed her in little more than a year and she surprised herself by her own self-restraint. If Mike respected her, he would tell her where he had been without her having to ask. If he didn't, she would soon find out.

Stella was the only person she could talk with on the matter. She would have been too ashamed to tell her mother and she didn't want to 'diss' the black man in front of Kathy and Rachel. What would they know? She needed to speak to her girl, but Stella was in California, visiting Lee.

The next morning she actually forgot that it was her own birthday. She got out of bed, thinking that in four months time, they would have been living in the farmhouse for a year, one anniversary she didn't wish to celebrate. She went downstairs and after changing into some outdoor clothes, walked the short distance to the bottom of the driveway where their postbox was. There were three birthday cards. One from her mother, Stella had sent one from California and the third one was from—Campbell Clarke?!

24% of black men learned their sexual technique from sexual partners, 17% learned from conversations with male friends, 13% from TV, films, radio or videos, 18% from sex manuals, text books or technique books, 13% from conversations with female friends, 7% from sex education at school, 6% from other, unspecified sources, and 2% from conversations with their parents.

NINE LIVES

Campbell sat alone in his loft apartment on the South Bank overlooking the Thames, dressed in a Santa Claus outfit. He looked at his watch, he had a few minutes more before he had to make a move. He sipped at his peach iced tea Snapple and admired the dustless bleached-wood floors of his apartment. He looked around the loft proudly—the stereo equipment, the stacks of reggae and jazz CDs, the large bowl on the coffee table filled with coconuts, oranges, and bananas, the huge punching bag in the corner of the massive living area. And then he thought of Dionne. She was, after all, the one he had decorated it for, who he had furnished it for in the hope that one day, however far-fetched, it would belong to both of them. Campbell often become so engrossed with thoughts of her that sometimes it was hard to function. To the outside world, he had his life together. To everybody else he was a successful black businessman who had got to the top, but inside, his soul was torn with torment by the futility of devoting himself to an unachievable goal.

So many times he had seen her come through that door and fall into his arms. It had seemed so real, he could touch it. Even though it was just his imagination, his heart had fluttered with emotion. He had expected to eventually get over her, but the memories of her refused to fade away. If only he could turn back the hands of time.

Campbell's first reaction when he heard that Dionne had

married Mike Phillips was to shrug his shoulders thinking, well hell, it's her loss. She could have had a great time with me and one day I'm going to make sure she regrets it. One day, when he was rich and successful, he would drive over to see her in a Rolls Royce and invite her to stay on his yacht moored at Chelsea Harbour. Then she would see.

That was his first reaction. It didn't take him long to want to get in contact with her. Through driving Valerie Owen, he was able to hear the latest updates on Dionne. He learned that she was happy in her new home in Sussex and that she was becoming pretty domesticated. He heard that she rarely came up to town any more.

Campbell couldn't understand it. He had all the wealth in the world and the one thing that eluded him was satisfaction. It was crazy; people spend all their lives dreaming about wealth and when they get it they don't know what to do with it. There were people out on the street who didn't have one percent of the wealth he had, yet they had much more loving than he had. It seemed so unfair.

He was tired of being alone...so, so tired of it. He had been on his own, without any real love, for years now. As much as he loved his loft apartment—it was the home he had always dreamed of—he was tired of coming home to a cold and empty place. He was tired of lying in his bed, wrapped in at night, dreaming about her. Not a single day had gone by since he last saw her when Dionne didn't feature in his thoughts and not a night had passed without her taking centre stage in his dreams.

He no longer had a problem remembering his dreams. They were too vivid in his mind in the mornings to forget. They were sweet dreams. Dreams from which he felt very good. They weren't exactly wet dreams, but he couldn't deny that they had a sexual element to them. And for some reason he always emerged from a night of beautiful dreams feeling as if he and Dionne had just spent the night together.

147

It was the season of goodwill to all men, but the sight of a black man dressed as Father Christmas and driving a criss new luxury car caused pedestrians to fall about laughing as they pointed to him, while other motorists were tooting their horns in jest. Campbell didn't mind though, it was the third year in a row that he was taking on the role of Father Christmas for the children in the home.

He drove through the old neighbourhood, he hadn't been there in a year, and memories came flashing back…bittersweet memories of hard times and all the stress of ghetto living. He had grown up in the roughest part of Hackney, where you could get jumped on in a minute if you looked at someone the wrong way, because as far as some of those youths were concerned, their neighbourhood was all they had to be proud of and they didn't want anyone distressing it. Campbell recalled that world, his world, as he drove down in his new Jaguar XJR. He had come a long way, and he was going further.

Sometimes he had to pinch himself when he realised just how large he was livin'. It didn't seem real to him. He didn't feel any different, but suddenly he had all this money and all this power and the way people responded to him was like he was not the same person he had been before. But no matter how much money he made, he was still a dollar short of satisfaction.

The newly registered Jaguar swung a right onto Sandringham Road and made its way up at slow speed. It wasn't often that Campbell managed to make it up to this side of town, now that he lived down by the river, but when he did, it always brought back memories. He glanced at where the frontline used to be. The group of run down shops outside which most of the players in Hackney used to congregate had long been torn down and replaced with newer buildings and there was now a mini police station where once there had been hustlers.

He had come further than most since his teenage days on the rough streets of his borough. Now he was a high roller like those stars he used to dream about whenever he flicked through the pages of *Ebony* magazine, stars whose pictures used to hang on his bedroom wall, way back when he used to have to juggle to survive. Now he was in the limelight and getting paid too.

Back then he wouldn't have imagined that he would be living in an apartment overlooking the Thames, and driving his own brand new Jaguar. He remembered when he used to have to eat sardines for dinner and even though he could now afford salmon, he would never forget those tough early days, when Christmas always seemed to miss him. Round here it was all about respect. Especially when you were a youth. There were too many people out to disrespect you. They'd call you a batty bwoy just for the fun of it and if you didn't punch them in the mouth and say, 'No, I'm not a batty bwoy', they would keep picking on you.

Even in school, it seemed as if the teachers were out to diss you, just because you came from a poor family in a poor neighbourhood. He remembered one time when his father had gone up to the school to sort out some problem his son had been in and the headmaster informing him that Campbell was more likely to end up being a mugger on the streets than make anything of himself. If only those teachers could see him today.

Halfway up Sandringham, he did a left and headed towards Dalston Lane.

If it wasn't for Valerie Owen, Campbell wouldn't have got out of that jail in the first place after the riots. He used up his 'one call' to phone her and tell her his predicament. She was

149

only too keen to come down and bail him out. The first thing she asked him was what he had done. He said he hadn't done much.

"We didn't all want the violence," he told her, "but if someone strikes you, what are you gonna do? Walk away? If you hit back, things might change. It's a chance we had to take. All these black leaders say we need to come together and pray for peace and hope, but we've got to more than hope the police are going to stop murdering us. When you're done praying and hoping and petitioning and marching, and they still ignore you, you've got no choice but to pump up your fist."

Eventually, Campbell admitted that he had cussed an officer, but that was it. "Everything else they're trying to stick on me is a frame-up."

"Are you telling me the truth?" Valerie asked, looking very serious. "Because I'm sticking my neck out for you. The papers would crucify me if it was discovered that I used my influence to get a guilty man off."

But Campbell was telling the truth, and the lawyer she appointed on his behalf was able to prove as much in court. He was, nevertheless, given a hefty fine.

Fat Freddy's death had really shaken the Black Men United crew. Nobody felt like joking and for the next few weeks, sessions at the sauna were a sombre affair. Gradually, they all started to come to terms with it and started remembering the good times with Freddy, and all his jokes. It was as if Freddy wasn't dead at all, but right there with them, when they vividly recalled the way he was.

It was Trevor who came up with the idea of going into a little business together. Campbell was all up for it. He had made a little money from a national newspaper after he had tipped them off about the white dude who used to hire him to drive while he was getting a blow job from a prostitute in the back seat. To his surprise, he had seen the man's photo plastered all over a poster for a new film. It turned out that the man was a well-known actor called Eugene Plant, who had a penchant for black whores. Campbell got a four-figure sum for the tip off, every penny of which he was prepared to invest in a business.

"Cars, man. That's what we've got to get into."

"Cars?"

"Yes, secondhand cars. You can pick up a secondhand car over here for next to nothing, then ship it to West Africa—to Nigeria, where even the trashiest cars sell for quite a bit of money."

Sometimes the simplest ideas were the best ones. They couldn't go wrong. With the money they pooled together, Campbell was able to travel to Belgium, Holland and Germany, picking up left-hand drive vehicles cheap— Benzos and Peugeots mainly. It also turned out that Ruffy and Tuffy were born in Nigeria and had family and contacts out there. The idea was getting better and better. Trevor flew to Lagos with the twins where they hooked up with a cousin who was reliable enough to act as an agent to look after the African end of their operation. Business was rough in the first six months, hampered by everything from customs to rip offs. But after that initial bumpy start, they did a roaring trade, shipping two cars a week to Lagos for the seemingly unlimited number of eager customers. Now, in their third year they were shipping 100 cars a week and had even bigger plans.

Campbell loved the life he was living. *Damn right!* It was all good. He had gone from negative to positive. There wasn't a damn thing positive about being poor. No black man was happy being poor. He had proven to himself that he could achieve anything he wanted to achieve and he had the money to make everything good. The only thing that money couldn't buy was someone to share it with.

He parked up outside the large Victorian house in Stamford Hill and pulled the big sack filled with presents out of the boot before walking up to the door and ringing the bell.

"Who is it?" he heard a chorus of expectant young voices shout from the other side.

"Ho ho ho!" Campbell roared in his deepest voice. "It's Santa Clarke and I've got presents for all the children who have been behaving themselves."

"Why didn't you come through the chimney, Santa?" a tiny voice called.

"Because I'm the black Santa and I always use the door. Ho ho ho!"

The door opened and a quintet of delighted children greeted him, each one eager to see what Santa had brought them. They surrounded Campbell right there on the doorstep and refused to allow him to move an inch until he had revealed the contents of his bag and handed them out. The excitement was understandable, because until three years ago, when 'Santa Clarke' appeared on the scene, these children had never enjoyed a Christmas. Whether or not the rest of the world cared about them, they knew that their black Santa would never forget them. And why should he? It was this same children's home which had taken Campbell, when as a young teenager, the social services had discovered him sleeping rough on the streets.

Campbell stayed at the home a couple of hours. It was worthwhile to hang around and see the children's happy faces enjoying their presents. There were all sorts of gifts, toys for the younger children and CD players and walkmans and a computer for the teenagers and a pair of the latest trainers for everybody. It really made Campbell smile to see the overjoyed expression on 7-year-old Martin's face when he unwrapped his trainers and saw that they were the exact pair he wanted with with a little pump attached for the air in the soles and a bright red light which shone with every step he took. He had a look on his face which said that he was the proudest, happiest boy in the world.

"I'm never going to take these off," he promised Campbell. "I'm going to wear them to bed every night."

As a way of saying thank you, little Martin went and got his crayons together and drew Campbell a festive greeting card with his crayons.

Smiley, so named because he had the biggest smile in the area, was equally delighted with the laptop computer Santa had brought him for Christmas. At seventeen, he was the oldest boy in the home and had been there the longest, because he was the kind of black youth potential foster parents hated to love—sixteen stones of beef, eyes that seemed too close together and curly hair that was tight and glistened with a touch of Dax. At the previous home he was in, the supervisor had even told him not to expect to even find a family, because "You've got too much black on. You look like you're in a gang."

Before he departed after a couple of hours at the home, Campbell took time out to exchange some words with Smiley. "So how are your A Levels going?"

"Don't worry 'bout that Santa," Smiley said with a cheeky grin, "everyt'ing cook and curry."

"So you're confident you're going to pass?"

"Yeah man."

"Well, we'll see in six months time, if you've thrown yourself in your studies enough for us to consider you an 'intellectual'. Have you had any offers from universities yet?"

"Yeah man. Bristol. They're asking for an 'A' and two 'B's. But maybe I'll stay in London. They want three 'B's."

Campbell nodded, satisfied. "Just remember one thing, that computer isn't for playing any games on, it's supposed to be for your essays. Yeah?"

Smiley nodded. "You think I've got time for games? You got to be kidding, man. They give us 'nuff work at college."

They punched fists, and Smiley followed him to his car.

"Just one thing, don…" He had that cheeky grin on his face. "Can you help me out? I'm a little light, can you spot me?"

Campbell instinctively went for his wallet. But then he thought better of it. People were always trying to tax him for his papers, and while he didn't mind giving ends to his friends, he didn't want Smiley getting into that beg, steal or borrow cycle.

"Cho'! What do you think this is, a game?"

"But we're like family," Smiley protested, still grinning.

"Lemme explain something. This isn't Monopoly, kid. This is something you don't learn in school. Cash rules. What you need is not necessarily what you get. Money talks, bullshit walks. If you want money, you've gotta work hard for it. Make your own help."

With that, Campbell drove off.

One of the best things about having wealth was being able to help your friends and family. He and Trevor had employed several of their homies—Ruffy and Tuffy dealt with the buying of cars and had become experts at picking up good deals on cars all over Europe, Bucky and Mikey arranged the shipping and booking of containers on cargo boats and Mark, who had now been disbarred from the legal profession since being convicted of assaulting a policeman at the Brixton riots, advised them on all the legal aspects of making sure that documentation of vehicles was in order and that all money transfers and import requirements were met. The whole crew were sharing in the success of Clarke Cars.

More importantly, with the money he now earned, Campbell was able to swallow his pride and make up with the father he hadn't seen for eighteen years. He had bought the old man a crib down in Portugal, where he could enjoy the sunset of his years in peace.

As Campbell drove home, he remembered something he needed to do and that was to send a Christmas card to a very important person. He took Martin's picture from the dashboard and considered it. Hand-made greeting cards were all the rage nowadays. And with its Christmas tree and matchstick people, Martin's picture was a special card. He pulled up outside a newsagents and got a stamp and an envelope and popped the card, addressed to Dionne's Sussex home, in the post box.

Valerie Owen had given him her daughter's address in the countryside over two years ago when Campbell had indicated that he wanted to send her a birthday card. He couldn't think of any other way to remind a married woman of who he was and that he still thought about her. It had been more than three years now since he last saw her.

He carried on driving Valerie Owen, even though he had long given up his job at Xecutive Cars and no longer needed the money, just as a way of keeping a tenuous link with Dionne. Trevor couldn't understand why he felt it necessary to chauffeur and was forever teasing him. But Campbell had his reasons and Trevor had learned to live with it. Mrs Owen was happy to talk about her daughter. The only person she never seemed to talk about was her son-in-law.

Campbell had thought about Dionne most mornings for the last three years. His memories of the snatched moments with her all that time ago were like jagged jigsaw pieces tossed about in his memory. In some ways his success was all down to her. Because when things got really rough and he felt as if he wasn't going to make it and he wanted to jack it all in, an image of Dionne would form in his mind and he was quickly reminded of his goal. He would probably have succeeded without it, but everyone needs a driving force.

Needing her was stimulating, the more he needed her the harder he worked. There was nothing else to do when you were in love with a woman that you couldn't get…you couldn't speak to. Not in that way anyway. Not about how crazy you were about her.

Why did I let her slip through my fingers?

When a man loves a woman, *really* loves a woman, he can't keep his mind on anything else. Dionne was married and would remain that way. The best thing he could do now was find another woman. But every time he tried to forget her, a reminder would appear, deep down in his soul, an eternal flame burning forever, wherever he went, making sure that even if he couldn't get Dionne, the woman he wanted most to be with, he would never love anyone else either.

Many of the black men we contacted believe in having their cake and eating it. A small but distinctive group prefer to have somebody else's cake and eat it.

ON THE COUNT OF TEN

An Easter card came in the mail from Campbell. Dionne opened it. His cards always seemed to give her a lift. He was a good correspondent who sent cards for every occasion and never forgot her birthday or seasonal greetings. This time though, he had also sent a large 'Easter cheque' for the twins. She made a note to send him a thank you card.

She should have been happy. She had two lovely children and a good home. She played her part and tried to be as good a wife and mother as was possible. *So why am I increasingly resentful, and why do I feel that I'm not respected for just being me and that I constantly have to earn my husband's love?*

The phone went. It was Stella.

"What's up, girl? I haven't heard from you all week."

"Nothing much. How have you been?" Dionne replied.

"Can't complain. You want to make sure that all this country living doesn't make you forget your friends up in London."

"No risk of that. I've just been a bit busy doing nothing, that's all. So what's happening in the big city? What's the latest gossip? Who's bonking who?"

"Girl, don't you have anything better to think about out there?"

Dionne thought about it for a moment. "No, I don't think I do."

"Behave yourself! Anyway, that's not why I'm calling.

Did you get the treatment I sent you?"

"Yes, it arrived this morning. Great idea. It's really our story, isn't it? Me and you. I'm sure that it would make a great film. And 'Waiting For Mr Right' is a great title."

"Wait until I finish the screenplay. Then we'll really know if it's worth turning into a film. Girl, I'm enjoying writing so much, I can't wait to begin the next screenplay. I've got dozens of ideas for films. How about you?"

"What do you mean?"

"You're supposed to be writing a script as well, remember? You were going to send me your treatment to look at."

"Jeez, I haven't even started. I've been so tired, always tired. No matter how much I sleep."

"What's wrong girl, are you sick or something?"

"No, I feel fine usually. Just tired."

"Are you sure you're not pushing yourself too hard, girl?"

"How can I be? I don't do anything."

"Yes, girl. But you've still got to slow down. Your body might be taking things easy, but what about your mind? What about your heart?"

Dionne sighed. "There's no point in kidding myself, living out here is wearing me out. And Mike doesn't make it any easier. Things aren't getting better between us. I just need some breathing room."

"I know what you're saying, girl. I know how you feel. I feel like that myself sometimes. Girl, if I were you, I'd move back to London. Three years out there is enough."

Alone in the house, Dionne's mind soon drifted off into the realms of fantasy. They were always sexual fantasies, which always succeeded in putting her in the mood for some loving, some caressing, some sweet words of praise. She had no intention of lying there thinking about her husband. When she was this much in the mood she

159

fantasised about any other man and if someone had knocked on her door right that minute he would have probably got it all, as long as he came with a smile on his face and a bit of tenderness for her in his heart. Sometimes she felt guilty about these thoughts, but they were always there, waiting for her to conjure them up when she was at her loneliest. And when she felt low and unloved, she could call on her fantasy man to come and wash all her troubles away, and the next moment he would be there, lifting her out of her boredom and up to the bedroom where they would have the wildest and most thrilling sex.

Rural life seemed to have no beginning and no end and Dionne felt completely isolated. She had listened to the Archers on the radio every day for over three years, and had read every good book in the house. She had spent countless hours at afternoon tea with Rachel and Kathy, watching TV talk shows and she now knew the difference between Oprah and Vanessa and Rikki Lake and Montel Williams—she knew them all. But she wanted something more to occupy her time when her 3-year-old twins were away at the nursery. Now every day was like a repetition of the previous day and you either enjoyed it and totally forgot about everything that was happening in the wide world, or you wouldn't be able to take it. And even though she had tried many times, Dionne couldn't forget about life in London and all her friends there. She missed going shopping with Stella and missed all the parties and going to the theatre any time you wanted to. Her worst mistake, she concluded, was allowing Mike to talk her into moving out into the wilderness.

Hadn't she told him that she would not become a housewife? Hadn't he promised her that she wouldn't have to become one? Well, what was she now? Just another one of those suburban housewives in the stockbroker belt who were staying at home waiting for their husbands to come

160

home every evening.

Mike didn't seem to care how she felt. As far as he was concerned, all that glittered was gold and his wife since they married had lost her shine. He had even had the nerve to ask her how come she was getting uglier. He was too preoccupied with his life to notice that she had stopped wearing make-up because she got tired of wearing it for the TV screen every night, while the only reason to make herself beautiful was working overtime.

She spent long hours thinking about her marriage, most of those hours thinking about her husband and how he had faded away, slipped away from her. Where had his love gone? Wasn't marriage supposed to be so wonderful? Wasn't it supposed to represent the happiest days of your life?

She could play the roles required of her, but inside she was frustrated by the domesticity of her life. She had married because she wanted to be married. She wanted stability, security and the words of a man telling her how much he loved her every day. But she also wanted excitement.

"Why can't marriage be exciting?" she had asked Mike when he came home late one evening and flopped down on the sofa in front of the TV without barely a word to her. Mike had started drinking a lot. As soon as he came home any night, the first thing he would do was plonk himself down in front of the TV and pour himself a large scotch, sometimes with ice, sometimes without.

Unfortunately, he could not accept the fact that his wife was suddenly questioning the validity of her way of life and instead of anything being resolved, they had got into an argument.

"What more can I do?" he protested. "As it is I'm working my bollocks off to keep you in the good life you're accustomed to. You think that money grows on trees? What more do you want?"

"Don't you know? Do you really not know?"

"No I don't."

"Well, let's start off with a little consideration for your wife when you're not coming home. A little phone call would put my mind at ease and I'd be able to sleep easily."

"So I came home a little late. Big deal."

"It's been almost two days."

"Yeah, yeah, yeah. So what?"

"I called you twice on your mobile."

"You called me once."

"Once, twice, thrice...whatever. I left a message. Why didn't you call back?"

"Look Dee, I'm not in the mood for any useless conversations tonight. I'm tired, I've had a long day. I just want to chill out. Okay, so you're heartbroken and you're sitting around feeling neglected, what did you expect out of marriage anyway?"

He poured himself another large scotch and sat staring at the TV screen without any of the images registering, preferring to be comatose than have to face his wife.

With every word he uttered Dionne's love for Mike diminished. If he knew what it felt like when the magic had gone out of a relationship you still believed in, he would have seen through Dionne's brave face and realised that her heart was crying for something more than this life, the life she'd been chained to.

"Baby, there's no need to talk to me like that. If something's bugging you, be a man and discuss it."

"What a load of nonsense," said Mike, exasperated. He didn't even want to argue the point, he wanted to sleep. He had had a hard day, and had come home to get a meal, to have a shower and to put his feet up for a minute before going to bed, he didn't come home to get into some nonsense argument with his wife. What was wrong with her that she had to always stress him like this and be so confrontational? Something had possessed her and he was determined to quash it whatever it was.

"All I'm asking for is a little respect, when you come home," Dionne pleaded. "Just a little bit, just a little bit. I'm the woman you married, remember? The mother of your children. The woman you profess to love."

"What's love got to do with it?" Mike asked with a sneer.

"It's got everything to do with it, I wouldn't be here if it wasn't for love."

"Bull. All you're interested in is what I can provide for you. That's why you married me. You wanted a man with power and position and that's who you got. If you wanted anything else you should have married that delivery boy of yours from Hackney."

"I don't know what you're talking about."

"Well I don't know what *you're* talking about."

Dionne sighed. She shouldn't have bothered, but she hoped that he might stop and think for a minute.

"Did you ever feel so depressed you didn't know what to do? Like you were living all of your days in darkness, feeling like somewhere, somehow, you lost yourself, and if you didn't get help quick you wouldn't make it through the day? That's how I feel, Mike. What are you going to do to help me?"

"Damn, I haven't got time to sort out your mind. Sounds to me like you're going to need some psychiatric help if you keep on talking like that. No wonder I never want to come home."

"And if you keep on talking like that, our marriage is surely going to end."

Mike shrugged his shoulders. "We'll cross that bridge when we get to it."

"We're already there! Can't you see that our marriage has been going steadily downhill? We've only been married for three-and-a-half years, but it feels like a lifetime. Because every week, no, every day, it gets worse. What happened to all the good times? We don't talk like we used to. There was a time when you used to say that you liked nothing better than lying in bed with me every Sunday and just talking. You used to say that you looked forward to it so much that it was what kept you going through a hectic week at work. And we used to laugh and joke all the time."

Mike glared at her and said, very slowly and deliberately, "You're selfish, you know. You've got no consideration for the fact that it's my behind on the line at the bank every day. That doesn't matter to you. Meanwhile, everything is running smoothly in our marriage and with the family, and just because you're bored or whatever at home, you turn to me. Dee, make your own help if you need it that bad." He kissed his teeth dismissively. "You don't know your own good fortune."

"Work, money. It always comes down to that with you, Mike. You think just because you work and bring in the money, that you can behave as you want to. I've told you several times that I can go out and work too. I want to go out and work. If you're so stressed at work, then tell me about it. I'll comfort you, but you never share any of the worries of work with me. Your work is like another world to which you disappear at 7.45 every morning and where you spend most of your life. I'm willing to take total responsibility for running our home, our finances and our family life. And I can do it all without you. Think about it Mike, me and my babies can manage without you if we have to."

Mike sneered. "You have to look in the mirror sometime and see who you really are. Because you're not who you think you are, believe me. You think you're a white woman, but you're not. Take a good look at yourself, you're black. As black as the ace of spades and you ain't going to get any lighter. I don't care how much money your mama's got, as far as I'm concerned you're always going to be black. No matter if you're better than I am, you're still going to be black. Think about it."

Dionne went to bed that night with a heavy heart. Mike had become so cocky, acting like he had all the answers to everything. What she hated most was that Mike stifled every opportunity she had to express herself and now he was trying to make out that he was some 'white' knight in shining armour and she was some piece of trash. Any black person who wasn't earning as much money as he was was, in Mike's view, common. But he seemed to forget the fact that his skin was black too, and no matter how much money he had that would never change.

He didn't care, or totally ignored the fact, that she had needs, wants, desires and other things that she cared about. In fact, when she thought about it, he didn't seem to care much about anything she did with the exception of the children. *His* children as he always called them, as if he had carried them for nine months, as if he had gone into labour and given birth to them and spent all the time that was needed to bring them up as she had done.

When was the last time that they had gone out for an evening meal together, or anywhere for that matter? Except for spending Christmas at her mother's place, they no longer went anywhere. Why had she married so hastily? Yet she clung tenaciously to her mistake, hoping against hope— for the sake of the children—that their marriage could be salvaged. And, even though their happy home was irreparably damaged, how could she leave Mike without causing a lot of pain to her children?

How could I have fallen in love with him ?

Dionne was still awake when she heard Mike staggering upstairs, but to avoid any confrontation she closed her eyes and edged as far away from his side of the bed as possible. She heard him fumbling about in the darkness of their bedroom, she heard his breath coming in short sharp alcoholic pants as he undressed and slipped into the bed beside her. At first he turned his back to her and pulled more of the blanket over to his side, pretending to sleep. Within a few minutes, however, she felt a cold hand snake up her thigh until he got to her crotch where his fingers fumbled about roughly and fruitlessly for the spot which would put her in the mood. After a few minutes of caressing her 'clitoris' he turned around, and, breathing alcohol in her face, soaked her face in sloppy wet kisses. She felt revolted.

"So you see I love you so much," Mike whispered in the darkness, fondling her breasts roughly. "There's no need to be so angry, there's no need to be in a bad mood, 'cause daddy loves his mama."

He could have said sorry, he knew he had done her wrong. Instead, he pushed himself deep inside her and started pumping away like there was no tomorrow. Dionne lay there still, listening to her husband's mutterings as he meandered through the ritual that carried him to orgasm. All the while, she was mentally ticking off the number of things she had to do the next day, her mind screaming silently as she felt her soul being violated with every thrust. The thrill had gone out of their loving and she couldn't wait for the moment when Mike exploded with a moan of painful pleasure and flopped down on top of her exhausted.

They lay like that, in the darkness, for the next fifteen minutes, with tears streaming down Dionne's face like a rain-swollen river as shame ate into her. It was slowly sinking in. She didn't want him and she didn't love him. She was through with being his fool.

"You don't have to say you're sorry," she said bitterly. "You don't have to say you're sorry, but I wish you would."

Mike snored loudly in reply. He had already slipped into a deep slumber.

This was a story with only one possible ending. Divorce.

46% of black men believe that they are 'God's gift to women'.
54% wish they were.

ELEVEN GOOD MEN

Though Black Men United no longer met up at the sauna as regularly as they used to, Campbell would hire out the entire Holloway pool on the first Sunday of each month, when it was otherwise closed, so that he and his crew could still take a sauna together and catch up on what was new and chat about old times and think about Fat Freddy. It was a pretty relaxed session where they could bring their own brew and several of the old crew would show up.

Mikey and Bucky were there discussing the success of their recently-launched pirate radio station which Trevor and Campbell had helped them fund. By all accounts they now owned the airwaves in London, playing real hip hop, ragga and jungle, but not the commercial stuff. Each show on the station was like a party, a continuous jam that was open to a million listeners—from the jeep posses cruising the West End, to the night watchmen working weekends, to the loyal followers locked in the Scrubs, Brixton and Pentonville. They played the music people loved.

Once Campbell and Trevor had succeeded in business and showed the others it could be done, they instilled confidence in their friends to spread their wings and fly too.

Ruffy and Tuffy were also living large. They had formed their own security firm, Rottweiler Security, an agency which provided bouncers for many of the West End clubs. Both were sporting a row of gold teeth. Their business was obviously doing well.

Trevor took Campbell aside. "Man you were on my mind all night long…I couldn't get you out of my thoughts, man. There I was, trying to have a wet dream and you're bugging me out on all of them…I've been thinking man, you really need to get yourself a woman."

Campbell sighed. Not this old chestnut again. Would Trevor never give up?

"No, hear me out, I was thinking, you've got all this money and everything, but you know you're not going to live forever, right? You're gonna have to start preparing for what's going to happen to the business when you go, man. You need an heir…believe man, you don't want to go out without any pickney. I was thinking of old Fat Freddy and how he passed away without any youths whatever. It would have been easier for everyone if he had left a child after him, you know what I mean? You think that you're going to live forever, but I've got news for you, homes, you're not. So you've got to make your decisions about life quick time. We're all going to die eventually and you never know, you could be walking down the road one day and, splat, an articulated lorry crushes you."

"Thanks a lot."

"But I'm serious, man."

"How many times do I have to tell you? When I get the right woman, I'll be having kids all over the place. Trust me."

"The right woman? The right woman. It's always got to be the right woman with you. What's wrong with you? You philosophise about this thing too much. You should just get a woman, man. Any woman will do right now. I know some really cool sisters out there who would be perfect for you. You're just the type of man that they want and they would go crazy over you. Which gal wouldn't? You're an eligible bachelor. You're good looking, you're young and rich and, most importantly, you're not a baby father. When you meet these girls I'm talking about, you're going to want to have some babies with them, believe."

"Why is it always that when you see a woman and a bed, you start wanting to test the bedsprings?"

Trevor laughed. "Because love is too painful for my sensitive nature. And besides, I thought it was the other way around."

"Women don't want to test out the bedsprings, they want to test the man," Campbell retorted. Anyway, there wasn't going to be any testing of anything tonight, he decided.

But Trevor insisted. "Just come for the ride."

Campbell thought about it for a moment. *Oh, why can't I just play it like a player? Like Trevor, like Sweetbwoy, like all the rest of them? Just take what's offered to me and not think about it so much.* He was never going to get any peace from Trevor unless he came correct with his spar.

"Man, I'm only interested in one woman. And I can't get her. I know it's crazy but my heart just isn't into other women. You know how a woman can get under your skin and whatever you do she's still there, messing up your mind?"

"Which woman's that?"

"Dionne."

"You mean that same woman from way back? Maaaan, forget it. She's married. You haven't got a chance there."

"I know, man. You don't think I don't know that? But knowing is one thing, you try and tell my heart to forget it. It just ain't that easy. I wish I didn't feel this way, but I do. I wish I could just go and check any woman. It would make my life so much easier. But it's like every woman I meet, I end up comparing to Dionne and they don't match up."

"Damn," Trevor said, looking impressed. "She must have given you some good loving back in the day."

"That's just the crazy thing, we didn't even get it

together."

"What?!! But I thought…"

Campbell shook his head.

Trevor started thinking. "So how long have you had these feelings for her?"

"All the time, man. I just can't figure out what to do about them. But I know that checking other women ain't going to do it for me."

"So when was the last time you checked gal? I mean *checked* gal? When was the last time you *really* dealt with a woman? You know, when was the last time you did the nasty?"

Campbell was embarrassed.

"You're talking ancient history, man. Do you remember the days of slavery?"

Trevor whistled. Had it been that long?

"But don't worry about that," Campbell continued. "I can deal with that, as long as there is the slightest hope that I'll get her some day."

"So what are you going to do, just kick back until she decides to get a divorce?"

"Something like that."

Trevor shook his head sorrowfully.

"Man, you're crazy, you know that Clarkey? You're pussywhipped and you ain't even had the pussy. What's wrong with you? There are guys out there who don't have two pounds to rub together and would love to be in your position right now, where you've got the digits to have any other woman you want. Okay, so you can't get Dionne. Look how many other women there are out there, while you're chewing over the card that fate has dealt you. But so what? You're a ghetto yout', Clarkey, you came up the rough way in the school of hard knocks and made it. Now, when you've got all the money you can spend and all the power that goes with it, you're still unhappy. What the f…?" Trevor kissed his teeth. "It's pure slackness, man. You've got everything. Just look in your garage, man, there's a Jag there. Just look at your apartment man, how many people have ever seen a loft apartment that size in London? With a view of the river too. Damn, Clarkey, you've got so much paper you don't know what to do with it. You've got three accountants looking after your digits and even they can't hide enough of your stash to keep the tax man at bay. And look how much you've done for all your homies. Everybody around you is happy and bigging you up. It's all good. If you can't do anything about the situation, just enjoy the moment. Live your life to the fullness. Whatever will be will be, and if nothing happens just move on. You have a right to be happy."

"Yeah. You're right. But you can keep the rest of the world. If the most important thing is missing from your life," Campbell mused, "everything else is unimportant."

28% of black men prefer to make love in the dark. 24%
always make love with a light on. 48% have no particular
preference as long as the sex is good.

SENTIMENTAL REASONS

"Alright, get ready, we're going to work that body…And reach, two-three-four-five-six-seven-eight…stretch, two-three-four-five-six-seven-eight. Push, two-three-four-five…step, step and turn around…"

The group of ladies in fashionably bright leotards worked their bodies as best they could in time to the sounds of Janet Jackson in the large exercise hall of the gym in Chelsea.

Stella had told her friend on her first visit that she wanted them both to get into shape because Lee had finally finished his Phd and when he came home they were going to set a wedding date.

Encouraged by Stella, Dionne had begun to travel to London once a week for a thorough workout with her friend after which they usually went for a coffee and did some shopping together in town. Thus, Dionne had been coming up to London for four months now, and it was one appointment she always looked forward to. It was not only a chance to get toned up, but also an opportunity to catch up on the latest gossip and exchange chat.

"You're looking real good," Stella congratulated as they were leaving the gym.

Dionne didn't just look good, she felt good as well, and radiated sunshine as she always did whenever she escaped the monotony of the countryside and came up to town. She couldn't believe how much she had let her figure slip in the last four years. Now she stuck to a rigid keep-fit programme. As well as the weekly aerobics workout, she went for a run every morning as soon as Mike had gone to work, over the hills and dales of the countryside around their farmhouse.

"You should come up to town more often," Stella said. "Honestly, I don't know what you get up to out there in the wilderness. What do you do with your time out there?"

"I spend most of it wishing I was back in London," Dionne said with a grin as she dried herself.

"Well then, move back."

"It's not as easy as that, I've got kids to think of. Remember?"

"Well, bring them with you."

"What about my husband? My home?"

"If you're not happy down there, move back, don't take other things into consideration. If Mike's down with the programme he'll move back with you, if he's not then that's alright. Did I tell you I bumped into Princess Di down here the other day? We had a really great chat, honestly Dee, she's such a nice woman. Anyway, it's just like she was saying, no man is worth being miserable for, even if he is the Prince of Wales."

Every time Dionne met up with her best friend, the conversation generally got round to Mike. Stella didn't have time for him and blamed him for trying to cut her off from all her friends. She would use every opportunity she could to diss him in some small way or other, especially since Dionne had finally admitted that things weren't loveydovey at home.

"I know you too well, Dee. No matter what you say, I know that you're still a girl about town and that you want all the bright lights and excitement—same as me. And I know you must be going through a lot of pain being stuck out there in the middle of nowhere. Four years! You've got to ask yourself if the price of pain is worth it, Dee. If he wants to stay out in the countryside then fine, maybe there's nothing between you any more anyway. So, send him on his way…send him packing."

Dionne shrugged her shoulders and said that she was used to living out in the countryside now, that it didn't bother her any more. "I just don't want anyone accusing me of being a bad mother."

They were now sitting at a table outside a little cafe on King's Road. It had been an unusually mild autumn and the warm sun had kept the Chelsea cafe culture out on the pavements throughout October. Stella poured herself some more tea from the stainless steel pot.

"Who's going to accuse you? Mike? Screw him. He must be living in the dark ages if he expects his wife to sit at home looking after the kids while he's out at work having all the fun. If he wanted to marry that good old 'woman behind her successful husband', he should have gone out to the middle of the desert to find her, because things have changed around here and if he hasn't changed, get rid of him."

"I wish I could turn back the hands of the clock," Dionne said dreamily. "All I've been doing the last year is drowning my regrets in black coffee. If I could go back in time, I would do it all different, but hey, I can't. So I'm coping with it, for the sake of the children."

"Why do you always use that tired excuse? It hasn't got anything to do with the kids. It's your decision. The kids will live with it. If you're not happy with your husband, just get rid of him. Kick his ass out the door. Don't try to patch things up. What's the use? It's gone too far now. When being in love means being in pain, you've got to tear it up, throw him out, push him out," Stella said. It was the best advice she could offer her friend. "That's what divorce is there for, so that you can exit a relationship as easily as you entered it. If Lee came home from the States and grunted at me instead

176

of talking to me, I'd call his parents and tell them to come and take their baby back.

"Understand this, Dee, when it comes to love, there are winners and there are losers. What are you going to be? I've watched you change from a woman who loved life, who wouldn't take shit from any man, who was the life and soul of any party, into a country housewife. I've got to say it, Dee, you've changed a hell of a lot. Too much in fact. If he doesn't treat you well, there are lots of guys out there who would. There's nothing wrong with you, you're still as good looking as you always were and you're not even thirty yet."

"I really don't think I'm interested in replacing Mike with some other man. If I did he would have to be someone pretty special."

The two sat in silence for a while. Dionne taking in everything Stella had said. Her friend was right. She *had* become a very different person; the type of woman that she would have found weak many years before.

"Guess who I bumped into the other day?" asked Stella, interrupting Dionne's thoughts. "Remember that driver...you know, the one who drove us to the C. Riley party? Wow, it must be over four years ago now."

"Oh, Campbell."

"Yes, that's right. He was with this handsome friend of his, Trevor, who was trying to chat me up, but you know me, almost married and everything, I told him I was unavailable. But he's called me up and wants to take me to the pictures. I made it quite clear that it was strictly platonic."

Dionne smiled.

"Campbell was asking about you," said Stella.

"What did you say to him?"

"I said that you were always asking about him," she replied.

"You never!"

"Yes, I did. Why not? I figured I was doing you a favour. Anyway, maybe you had been asking about him. What do I know?"

Campbell Clarke. Dionne drifted into a sentimental journey back to the days before she got married. "So, what's he like nowadays?"

"Still a hunk," Stella replied with a twinkle in her eye. "He's still a driver though, driving Jaguars. He gave me his number. Hold on a second." She rummaged in her handbag and produced Campbell's business card. She handed it over to Dionne. "He said I should give it to you in case you've lost it…why did nothing ever happen between you and him anyway?"

Dionne thought about it for a moment. "Oh, he was never interested in me."

"You're kidding. He was crazy about you. I saw it in his eyes from the moment I first saw him. He hardly noticed me."

"If you say so. Anyway, back then you couldn't see me going out with a cab driver, could you…? Seriously."

"Oh I don't know. It's not what the man does that matters, it's how he treats you." Stella looked deep into her friend's eyes. "Look, he might be poor, but you would probably be happier with him than you are in your present situation. Take that number and call him."

Dionne said that she would think about it. Deep down, that was exactly what she wanted to do, but she knew she wouldn't. Too many years had passed. They probably wouldn't even recognize one another if they bumped into each other.

68% of black men claim they could spot Miss Right if she came walking down the street. 32% said they would prefer if a giant arrow descended from the sky and pointed her out to them.

Unlucky For Some

Like any mother who had struggled by herself to put food in her daughter's mouth, Valerie Owen would probably have been suspicious of any man who tried to stake a claim on Dionne. Whoever he was.

But when Dionne had come back from Acapulco, Valerie had learned of her agreement to have a joint bank account with her husband. This had worried Valerie. Why did they need a joint bank account? What had gotten into her head to make her so willing to sign away all that freedom?

"Love," Dionne had said. The joint bank account was a testament of their love for one another. "What's mine is his and what's his is mine."

Valerie could hardly believe her ears. *Is all that time and money I spent on educating this girl gone to waste?* Hadn't there been times when she also had met men and fallen in love without having a joint bank account? Hadn't she taught Dionne that you must use love and not the other way around? That it was never the other way around if you were a woman. And anyway, why did Dionne have to prove her love with a joint bank account?

But when young girls are in love it is impossible to make them see reason and Valerie had already made arrangements to insure her daughter's independence. So when Dionne had mentioned this, she had called up her financial adviser and given him instructions to block any transfer of money from Dionne's trust fund.

180

All of this had made her dislike Mike Phillips even more than she would have ordinarily. And, there was enough there to dislike already. Why was her daughter married to such a man? Her beautiful, intelligent, charming Dionne? To cap it all the idiot wasn't even making her daughter happy. She could see it on Dionne's face every time she came up to London. Dionne didn't have to say a word, she knew her daughter well enough to know her husband wasn't treating her right.

"Campbell…!" Valerie said next time they were in the car together, a thought crossing her mind.

"Mrs O," Campbell answered from behind the steering wheel of the Jaguar as he headed for her Hampstead home. "What can I do for you?"

There was no reply. Campbell studied the elegantly dressed black woman in his rearview mirror. She seemed to be lost in thought, her eyes staring right through him.

"Is everything alright, Mrs O?"

"What…?" the lady looked up. "Oh yes, Campbell…thank you. Everything is alright. Everything is just fine. I was just wondering…? No, it was nothing…"

"Are you sure, Mrs O?"

"Yes, positively. Thank you, Campbell."

"Any time Mrs O."

She didn't seem in the mood for a chat, so he decided not to bother her. He still enjoyed driving her, even though he could afford not to a million times over. He smiled to himself, wondering how long it would take her to twig that he was no longer the Campbell Clarke, cab driver of old.

"Mrs Owen…Mrs Owen?"

Valerie snapped out of her thoughts. Campbell had pulled up outside her house and was now standing with the rear door open, waiting for her to exit.

"Oh," she said, "we've arrived."

"Indeed we have Mrs O."

"Thank you so much," she said, taking Campbell's outstretched hand for support and climbing out of the car.

"Would you like to come in for a cup of coffee?" she asked him. "There are some things I want to show you."

"Coffee, Mrs O? That would be just fine."

He followed her into the house as he had done several times over the past years. A few times she had asked him to help her out with moving furniture from the attic upstairs and even with some DIY. It was true to say that over the years they had become friends, even if much of their discussion centred around their mutual interest—Dionne.

Mrs Owen pulled out a couple of large family albums and handed them to Campbell as he sipped on some hot, black coffee.

"I think you'll find these pictures interesting," she said.

Campbell started turning the pages of the first album, glancing over the early photos of Valerie and her late husband and then baby pictures of Dionne and others of mother and daughter both together and separate. The albums covered thirty years of Dionne Owen's life, right up to the present day with the final photos in the second album being of Dionne, looking as irresistible as Campbell had remembered her, with her twin daughters.

"What you have to understand, Campbell, is that my daughter and I are best friends, but Dionne was always a wild child who went her own way. I shouldn't have been surprised that she could run off and get married without telling me. You see, Dionne was a highly emotional child, who lived in a fantasy world," Mrs Owen said, reminiscing. "She used to have imaginary playmates with whom she engaged in some pretty wild and far-out games. By the time she was a teenager she was rebelling in any and every way. You name it, she would do it. She started smoking, staying out late, and generally trying to make me uncomfortable and unhappy, but I wouldn't admit it. You see, it wasn't until later...oh, when she was about fifteen, that I discovered what was at the bottom of it all. Even though she was only a child when her father died, she had a very strong memory of him. She even remembered exactly what he looked like—that he had a thick moustache and that he always wore a hat, even in the house. And even though I had explained to her about how her father died, she had harboured a belief that I had done away with him." She laughed at how ridiculous a notion that was. "Can you imagine? You see, that's why she was always falling in love from very early on, looking for a man who could replace her father. Her biggest fear was ending up like me, without a partner, and having to struggle to bring up her children. Despite being outwardly brash and in control she just wanted a conventional, fairy tale life with a good husband and 2.4 children. So she falls in love too easily instead. Even today, she can fall into a romantic reverie at the sound of her favourite song or sonata. You see, Campbell, the best thing we can do for our children is to make them feel very special early on in life. The reason I got into business in the first place was to be able to make Dionne feel very special. But money isn't always the best way to make someone feel special. Many other ways mean so much more."

Valerie Owen paused, lost in her own thoughts. Campbell nodded understandingly. Everything she had said was important to him and, he thought, might come in useful. Valerie turned to him and looked deep in his eyes.

"What's your game, Campbell?"

He almost choked on his coffee. "Game, Mrs O?"

"Yes, game. Why are you still posing as a cab driver? You obviously don't need the money any more. Something about you has changed over the last few years, there is something not quite right about why you're still driving me around after all this time. If you tell me what your game is, maybe I can help."

*44% of black men don't know if they are highly sexed, 32%
say they're not, and 24% say they are.*

Fourteen Play

One of the first things Lee wanted to do when he came home from America with his PhD was get married. He had longed and pined for Stella the entire time he was out there and now he was back he didn't want to waste any time at all.

"We've got a whole lot of loving to do," he told her and she agreed. It was time to start a family.

They didn't want an especially big affair, he would have been happy to have had just a few family and close friends. But by the time word got out about the wedding date, they were inundated with so many well wishers that their guest list just grew and grew and grew. Finally, Stella's mother had decided that they were going to hire an entire hotel near Brightlingsea on the Essex coast for her daughter's greatest day.

Dionne was one of the first to be told the date and, of course, she would be the maid of honour. Mike however, tossed aside his invitation and said he didn't know if he could make it. When the day finally came, he decided that he had better things to do.

So Dionne was there alone. Sitting in church, crying softly as she watched her best friend get married. Remembering that she herself was in exactly the same position a few years before and how she had felt when she was married in the little chapel in Acapulco. The memories came flooding back to her, of how optimistic she was about the future and how she had truly believed it to be the happiest day of her life, ready to give her husband more love than a man had ever known in his life. She kept thinking of Mike in his wedding suit and of the promises they made each other: to love and honour for better or worse. *So, this is the 'worse' they were talking about. I don't want worse, I want 'better'. I've got to make things better.*

She had felt nervous throughout the church service, when she had first noticed him looking across at her. And now they were seated at tables opposite each other during the meal. He was a friend of Lee's, but not close enough to be up on the main table.

It wasn't just the body language, he also knew how to send messages with his eyes which mesmerised and held her gaze, with promises of earthly delights beyond measure.

She had been sitting by herself, very self-conscious of the suggestiveness in the boy's eyes. Why couldn't she ignore him? Why was she having to drag her gaze away only to be drawn back in his direction and to be locked in eye contact? How could he force her to do something against her will?

He had been watching her for a while and he knew that she had noticed him. She wanted him, he was sure of that much. He carried on watching her, smiling, nodding.

She wondered if this was a game he was playing, a little game to which only she was party. Even when she looked away he would continue watching her from where he sat on the table opposite until she caught his eye and then he would fix his gaze on hers and almost hypnotise her until she could take it no longer and she had to break into a smile before looking away. He looked as if he was prepared to go on like that all night and it didn't bother her if he did, she would happily let him. For, if truth be told, she was enjoying it. She had all the time in the world and she intended to give him as much time as he needed.

She thought about the craziest things…but no, he was too young, what was she thinking? Sexual thoughts…a wild romp in bed…shedding all her inhibitions. She couldn't stop thinking about it and she knew that it was entirely up to her, all she had to do was say the word, and he would be hers. Then she thought of Mike at home with their daughters. How could she do this? Was this being a responsible mother? Why did it seem so easy?

They exchanged glances again. It seemed so conspicuous, but no one else in the entire place knew what was going on between them. It was like they were in a world of their own, exchanging intimate glances, little smiles and gestures. Maybe she was reading it totally wrong. Maybe he was smiling at someone else. Oh, where had that confidence she had once gone?

She would watch him watching her, but keep her distance. She had to keep away from him, otherwise Lord knows what might happen.

The meal over, the tables were removed and piled to one side to make room for the first dance. The sound system played some soulful music as the newlyweds stepped onto the floor. Dionne stood watching with everyone else, a tear rolling down her cheek as she saw her friend for the first time as Mrs Lee Perkins, looking lovingly into her husband's eyes as he held her in a gentle embrace. The look in Lee's eyes said it all, he was in love. Had Mike had that look in his eye on their wedding day? Dionne couldn't remember.

"Would you like to dance?" a voice breathed into her ear.

Dionne almost jumped with surprise. It was him, the man she had been exchanging glances with all afternoon. Though she was slightly flustered, she managed a smile and a nod. Like to…love to…it had been so long since she had danced, she wondered if she would be able to remember how. But this was a slow groove and that was one dance that you don't forget.

"Your flirting is getting me so aroused that I'm having difficulty concentrating on polite conversation," the boy said as he led her to the floor.

It wasn't the first time Dionne had heard that line, but this time it didn't sound as cheesy as it had previously. On the dancefloor, he took her gently by the waist and they danced slowly, seductively, on and on and on...

They continued like that for most of the evening, not saying anything, just dancing, locked in each other's gaze. It wasn't until much later that Dionne realised they had been dancing together for hours and only then did she realise that she didn't even know his name. That's how it is when dancing is so good and you are lost in another world—the world of your fantasies.

He said his name was Eric. She had never liked the name before but somehow it suddenly sounded poetic to her. He was actually twenty-five but looked younger. That didn't matter to her, as long as he didn't have the brains of a teenager. They laughed together. She was ashamed to admit it, but she was curious to find out whether Eric had as many moves in bed as he had on the dancefloor. Not that she would tell him that. She preferred to kick back and let him make all the moves. Twenty-five was still twenty-five after all and, what was more, she was still a married woman.

Dionne hadn't intended to have an affair. Even though there was no love, no passion, no romance left in her marriage. She had been loyal and steadfast and prepared to see her marriage through. But no longer. She was unloved and lonely. Now she needed someone to love her. The men she dated before she married may have been afraid of commitment, but being with them was better than being stuck in an unhappy marriage. The way she felt right now, she would have happily given the thought of marrying

Campbell Clarke her utmost consideration.

Oh damn the married woman bit. Why did that always have to come up? It wasn't as if she felt like a married woman any more. She felt more like a single mother, even, as much as she hated to use the words, a 'baby mother'! Her worst nightmare had always been to be considered in that way, but here she was openly taking on the term for want of a better way to describe how she felt in marriage. She was as lonely as any baby mother, as bitter as any baby mother and as in need of a good hug as any baby mother.

Eric, must have sensed how she was feeling right then, because just at her most vulnerable moment he whispered in her ear that he was really horny for her right now and suggested they take a walk on the nearby beach. Dionne went weak at the knees. That was exactly what she wanted to do, but how could she?

She laughed it off as if it were a joke. But the right words didn't come out. She wanted to say 'I'm a married woman', but what actually came out was, "You're attractive, you're charming, you're smooth and exciting...if I wasn't a married woman, I probably would, but..."

"The fact that you're married is not a problem," Eric replied as quick as a flash. "No one need ever know..."

"Mmmmn", her knees went weak again, her heart beat faster and butterflies danced about in her stomach...what was happening to her? She looked deeply in his eyes and wondered whether this boy was really saying what he was saying and whether he knew what he was letting himself in for, that she was a married woman who hadn't had any good loving in years and was truly, madly desperate for someone like him and she would milk him of all his sweetness in a moment if he just showed her the way to go.

She had forgotten what it was like to be seduced, what the sweetest things whispered in your ears sounded like and to have them said to you without you having to ask for them to be said. How had she allowed five years of marriage to deprive her of all these wonderful things?

Eric led her by the hand across the dancefloor to the front entrance of the hotel. Across the road was the beach and beyond that the ocean. They made their way over, Eric in total control, talking all the time.

"I see you're one of those ladies who likes to go to parties on your own," he smiled.

"No, not at all," she answered coolly. "Au contraire...it's just that I happen to be here alone and I've been drinking."

"You know what they say about women who drink alone," he continued, "they're not getting the loving they need."

How right he was.

"To be honest," Eric continued, "I never saw you as the kind of woman who was into men like me."

You'd be surprised, she thought, but didn't say. "What do you mean?" she asked.

"Well you know, I'm kinda cool and you're kinda square."

She slapped him on the head playfully and told him not to be cheeky.

"Take it easy...take it easy...there's no need to hurry, we can save the agony until later...no, I'm just wondering what a nice girl like you is doing walking on a beach, in the middle of the night, with a strange man. What would your mother think?"

"Well my mother's square, like your mother and like every mother, so she would think I was crazy. But fortunately, my mother's not here. She's back in London. And she may never know..."

Eric smiled. He said that she was truly amazing. "You have the most beautiful eyes..." He said there were so many good things he could say about her: she was attractive, intelligent, warm, charming. He fingered the pearl necklace around her neck admiringly. "You don't need jewellery, you're beautiful enough already."

The temperature rose to fever pitch. Dionne couldn't believe that she was imagining a love affair with this young boy.

They talked and talked and talked. Eric was teasing and exciting and sounded rough and ready, but listening closely Dionne realised that he was in fact quite intelligent and well-read. She didn't hear everything he said because her mind kept drifting to thoughts of sweetness as she watched his appetising lips moving slowly apart. Part of the time all that registered was the deep, husky, drawl of his voice which made him sound crazy, sexy and cool. Oh, what was she thinking? But she had already made up her mind and if he played his cards right, if Eric carried on the way he had been going so far, he would be getting off with her tonight. She was definitely in the mood, all he had to do was keep on pushing the right buttons.

"I can't understand certain men and how they behave," Eric said. "I mean, your husband, he doesn't deserve a woman like you...if I was your husband, I would give you so much sweetness you would never look at another man."

"Yes," Dionne sighed. She had had such dreams once, but those dreams seemed so faded now. "Me and my husband aren't getting on. But I don't want to talk about that right now. It's time I started doing my own living before I grow old."

She turned to him and smiled warmly, invitingly.

The stars were shining bright in the velvet sky above and the night breezes seemed to be whispering 'Go girl', as they walked barefoot on the sand.

"The place is here and the time is right for fireworks tonight," Eric announced when they reached a secluded part of the beach. Dionne looked around furtively. There was not a soul in sight. Eric took off his jacket and lay it on the sand for them to lie on. Then he flopped down on it and patted the space beside him for her to do the same. Throwing caution to the wind, she lay beside him.

He kissed her once and then once more. A chill ran up her spine and then other thrills which she couldn't define, she felt like she was going to melt in his arms. She wanted it to be true. She had found another world, and she wanted it to be so real. She closed her eyes and asked him to kiss her again and then again and again, to make sure it wasn't going to disappear. Then she opened her eyes and looked up at his face, illuminated by the silvery moon. That was when it dawned on her that this was the point of no return.

"This isn't a good idea," she said, suddenly getting cold feet.

Eric stopped abruptly as he kissed her neck. He paused, then turned his head and looked straight into her eyes. What he saw there was passion, hot, uncontrollable passion. He smiled softly, with kindness in his eyes. Then he resumed his kissing, this time more passionately, with his extended tongue caressing the tip of her ear, his breath blowing in short breaths into her ear.

A "mmmmnn" escaped from Dionne's lips despite herself. *It…it's…sooooo good!* "Nooo….nnnooo…" she pleaded, "don't…please E…ric…don't."

She needed all her willpower to push him away, but she succeeded.

"Will you leave me so unsatisfied?" Eric looked dismayed.

Dionne laughed. "Unsatisfied?" she raised an eyebrow.

"Don't worry…" Eric assured her. "Just lie back…be happy…think of good things. I know what I'm doing. I've got forty four ways to make you feel good."

Again she gave in to him. He was caressing her, but really he was undressing her. His hand wandered up her blouse and one by one, she felt the buttons pop open, until all that remained between the heavens and her breasts was a flimsy brassiere. He licked her slowly down to her belly button, his hands massaging her bra and its contents expertly.

"Relax. When it comes to sex, I'm similar to the thriller in Manila," he grinned, sticking out a stiff tongue and probing further down. Her skirt buttons popped open.

*Oh well, the point of no return…*Dionne was thinking, her body rushing with adrenaline. She loved everything about the way he made love to her. She loved the way he squeezed her, the way he teased her…the way he whispered in her ear, the way he smiled at her, the way they hugged. And she loved the caressing warm summer breeze and the sound of the waves lapping close by. It was simply beautiful.

He lifted his head prematurely from between her legs and pulling out a condom from his wallet, he showed it to her.

"Now, close your eyes and see what else I've got for you," he said.

With a nervous smile, she did as he asked. She could feel her thighs quivering and she felt wet in her panties. She was falling to pieces with anticipation of sexual feelings she had almost forgotten about. The need for sweetness was killing her. How was it possible that this young boy could make her feel this way?

Right up until the last moment she didn't know whether she would go through with it. All the possible repercussions were staring her in the face. She started getting cold feet and in what sounded like a panic told Eric that this was the first time she had done this. He didn't hear at first as he was too busy sucking her nipples, which were now erect and hard.

"What?" he asked.

"I said, this…I don't usually do this…I don't want you to think I'm the sort of woman that cheats on her husband…"

Eric smiled at her reassuringly. He wasn't making up his

mind on what type of woman she was from the fact that they were making love. He thought she was just fine.

But she didn't seem to hear him...she was lost in her own little world of recriminations and fear.

"Nobody must ever know..."

"No, nobody will ever know," he reassured her. "Nobody."

Dionne lay her head back on the soft sand and allowed herself to enjoy as much as possible.

So intense was the lovemaking, that they both forgot that they were in a public place and just then, neither of them could care less if anyone was walking on the beach. Dionne was in a different world. She had discovered heights of pleasure she had forgotten she possessed and she whooped and screamed and yelled with excitement and passion, tearing at Eric's hair and begging him not to stop. But Eric was crying back, "I can't hold it much longer...I'm trying...I'm...I...oh no, oh no...ooooohhh yessssss, yesssss. YESSSSSS! Jeeeeeeeeeeeeezas."

"Nobody must ever know," she whispered, as he moved on top of her. "Nobody must ever know."

"I promise you, nobody will ever know."

They lay there for a while. Dionne thinking of all the wonderful things she was experiencing inside of her. She hadn't managed to climax herself, but it didn't matter. Not just now. An overwhelming feeling of release came over her. She had taken the first step. If Eric was as keen as she thought he was, he would have many more chances of getting it right for her. At the moment, she just wanted him to hold her tight and tell her that he would miss her until the next time they were together. He promised that he would, "No doubt about it."

"Good," she said. Knowing there was someone somewhere longing for her would get her through life with her loveless husband. Eric suggested that she should dream a little wicked, wild and wet dream about him at night whenever she was lonely.

"Thanks for the memories…" she told him, nibbling his erect nipples. "It's been a long time." She just wanted him to know that she was feeling right tonight.

In the distance, they could see a man walking his dog along the coastline. They suddenly remembered how exposed they were and quickly got dressed and started walking back towards the wedding reception.

"So when am I going to see you again?" Eric asked.

Dionne smiled. "Soon," she said. "Very soon."

Soon couldn't come fast enough for Dionne. She called Eric within a week on the mobile number he had given her. They arranged the details. She booked a room at a hotel of her choice in town and they met up there the next afternoon. Eric didn't keep her waiting.

They didn't waste any time, but went straight up to their room and undressed. Dionne wanted to feel loved again and Eric had every intention of satisfying her.

Locked in a tight embrace, they gave each other their all, while the air conditioning hummed softly in the corner of the room. When they could give no more, could take no more, they lay sweating on the bed exhausted.

"So tell me about your husband," Eric said, when he had recovered enough.

"Husband…no, I don't want to talk about him."

"Why not?"

"Because Mike doesn't have a clue what I want in life, because he's not interested in who I am any more. He thinks I'm still the same woman that he married, but I've changed and he hasn't taken time out to see who I've become."

"So why did you marry him in the first place?"

Dionne sighed. "Because I loved him. Because I was young and foolish. He was exciting and charming and had money to take me off to places girls only dream about, and he wanted to marry me, so in the end I just thought, oh sod it."

"So what happened?"

"I gave myself completely to him, I was a good friend and wife until he hurt me, humiliated me, and made me feel abandoned."

"I'd like to meet this man. He must have 'e-e-e-d-i-a-t' tattoed across his forehead."

"I wouldn't like you to meet him. Lovers and husbands don't go together."

"But he's got to be crazy. Anyone can see that you need a man who appreciates you. Someone like me who wants to put you up on a pedestal and treat you like a princess. Not just sometimes, but every day of the week. If you were my woman I would praise you all the time, worship you and serve and support you. Forever."

"Take it easy, Eric. I love being with you. But I don't love you. Let's not get heavy with this thing, let's just take it easy and enjoy our afternoons together."

Eric agreed reluctantly. He had no choice if he was going to carry on seeing this woman. He was going to have to take it one step at a time. Maybe someday…

It was always good with him, and even though her head said, 'watch out', her heart was saying, 'give in to him'. She was never the same again afterwards. It was like she was a new person and she waited excitedly, expectantly, for each new time they would meet.

That first illicit afternoon at the hotel was quickly followed by a second and then a third. It soon became a weekly rendezvous. Once a week, she would leave Imani and Noir with a nanny and travel up to London to check into a hotel—a different one each time to increase the excitement—where Eric would meet her and they would spend a good few hours together simply making love and exchanging words of love. It was what she needed and she was no longer ashamed.

Love had nothing to do with it. Dionne realised that. Eric made her feel comfortable and she wanted to see him as much for relaxation as for the sex, passion and affection. When they were together Eric gave her his undivided attention and was learning how to stimulate her. She wasn't getting it at home so she had gone out looking for it, or more exactly it had come out looking for her and it had found her, she was receptive to it.

Dionne laid down strict rules for their liaisons. There were to be no public displays of affection between them. And although she had given him her home number, just in case he needed to call her quickly for any reason, he had to remember the code.

"When you call, let the phone ring twice, hang up and then dial again. Call only if it's an emergency; if my husband answers, hang up." She didn't want Mike finding out before she was ready for him to find out, if ever.

Afterwards, she would take the train home again and revert to her role as mother and housewife. She had become a master at switching roles as quickly as a chameleon changes colours. From housewife to lover to housewife, she moved easily between the two with a quick flutter of her long lashes.

At first, she felt too guilty about her Wednesday afternoon visits to town to let anyone know. Even Stella. She knew Stella would understand and support her, but she was too riddled with guilt to confide in her.

Mike was too involved with his own life to consider why his wife was suddenly blooming and cheerful. He just wasn't interested.

He didn't have a clue what she was really doing. The furthest thing from his mind was that the wife he had married, and had now grown tired of, would be of any interest to somebody else.

Mike had become like a stranger to Dionne. They no longer shared each other's thoughts, and when she looked at him she could have been looking at any passerby on the street. With Eric, on the other hand, she was having a relationship of mutual admiration. Eric was there for her and prepared to lie back and take a passive role when the moment required him to do so. With him, she could realise those fantasies she had been afraid to share with her husband. And with Eric, there were no strings attached. She wasn't marrying him, she wasn't in love with him and she always had one eye on the door, in case the experience became dull or uninspiring.

And does size matter? Not according to 60% of black men.
21% say it does. 19% said "how would I know?"

SLOW AND SEXY

Mike Phillips was a man who loved nothing better than to hear his own voice. But as good as Mike was in boosting himself up, Trevor was better.

"When you've got a lot of money, everybody wants a piece of it. Sometimes I have to dress in just jeans and a sweat shirt when I go out to parties, because money attracts all the wrong sort of people. Where were they when I had to stick cardboard in the bottom of my shoes when it rained? I didn't see them then, but now that my pockets are fat they're all over me. Not just women, but guys, you know, grown men.

"Already I've got a hoard of old friends that I never knew I had, and ex-friends and acquaintances and acquaintances of friends of mine, all of them looking a bly. People who love to borrow, but have never heard the word lend. I'm tired of having to tell them 'no', that it's a harsh world. I just say, 'I can't do nothing for ya, man'. If they say they haven't eaten all day, I say, 'neither have I'. If they say they haven't got money to pay the landlord, I just give them the address of a good charity which takes in homeless people. It's not that I'm mean, you understand. Far from it. With my real friends my generosity knows no bounds. But these other people are just opportunists who would rather kick back and let me do all the work while they enjoy the fruits of my labour. They've got to get themselves off their backsides because anything I do for them financially just increases their dependence and they'll just keep coming back for more.

"The best thing about being rich though, is that a lot of pretty women rush you. You don't even have to be good looking, all you have to do is have a fat wallet and they'll fall at your feet. You see, when you've got as much money as I have, you've got to play it cool or you'll be working for the honeys. You know what I'm saying?"

Mike nodded. They were sitting in a basement bar in Covent Garden, having a few drinks, admiring a couple of seductively clad women looking in their direction. Normally, he wouldn't have bothered taking a lunch break, but Trevor Maclean was one of his most important new clients. A little eccentric perhaps, a result of being one of these Johnny-come-lately nouveau riche with very little good breeding. A ghetto boy made good and who wore a diamond studded Cartier watch gleaming beneath the cuff of his Savile Row suit. His shirt was pure Pierre Cardin and the rings on his fingers harboured the very biggest rocks. He even had a diamond in his tooth. A million dollar smile. Mike didn't care what his background was, the bottom line was he had money. Not only was he rich, he wanted to invest a large amount of money and had insisted on Mike, the only black broker at his bank, to represent him.

The diamond tooth was just another one of the extravagances that Trevor allowed himself now that he had more money than he knew how to spend. Like the Rolls, he didn't need the tooth but it looked good.

"The only reason I wanted to be rich when I was a kid was to get a lot of women. If every man had that on his mind, he would work twice as hard. It's the perfect motivation. You see me, I wasn't born with a silver spoon in my mouth. I'm a Hackney youth, I came up the rough way. I've worked digging ditches to earn corn, you know what I'm saying? When I was picking up that shovel with all blisters on my hand, the one thing that kept me going was that one day I was going to make it. I was going to make it big-time and then I would be surrounded by some of the world's most beautiful women. And that's exactly what's happened. But there's a payback—women are an expensive hobby, the more you've got, the more they cost.

"Now, half the women in London know about my Rolls Royce and the Rolexes and about jewellery. They even heard about the place I bought my mother out in Portugal. And now they want to take some of my digits. It's the girls that will kiss you and caress you and make love to you after the first night, they're the ones who are out to getcha. To tell you the truth, I'm into it...all that hype...all that sex. But I'm thinking of settling down. You know, getting married and everything. That'll keep all the gold diggers at bay. You're a married man, Mike, would you recommend it?"

"Well," he thought carefully, wanting to give the answer his client wanted to hear, "speaking as your financial adviser, I can quite categorically say that there is a cash incentive in getting married, you'll get some tax back. Not much, but then I'm sure you can afford not to take that into consideration. If you're asking me personally, I'd say marriage is like a business and like any business it's in a state of flux and every new day brings forth a new challenge...if I had my way again I would be single. Don't get me wrong, I love my woman and everything...it's just that if I had my way again I wouldn't have got married. Think of all the things you'll miss out on not being single. When you start adding it all up... you can't go out any time you want to, or come home any time you want to, without your wife being on your case. You have to decide whether you want to rule your life, or whether you want someone else ruling it. Because that's what marriage is all about. I thought I was marrying Miss Right, the perfect woman. She's attractive, sensuous, intelligent...all the things that a man like me needs. I decided that this was the woman I wanted to spend the rest of my life with and have children with, and I made a go of it. But now I'm finding that I barely have enough time to live my own life. I would leave her, if it wasn't for the kids."

Trevor sipped slowly on his beer as he listened. "So what's stopping you checking other women?" he asked. "That way you can have your cake and eat it. And your wife need never know."

Mike smiled and tapped his nose with his finger conspiratorially. "Between you and me, I haven't been a good boy all through my marriage. My wife's a bit dull and, you know how things are, working in London and living in the country. When the cat's away and all that."

Trevor gave him a knowing smile and then got up to use the bathroom. He returned a few minutes later with a young girl of no more than nineteen at his arm.

"Hey Mike, say hello to Tina." Trevor, a big grin on his face, introduced the girl. She had thick make-up and a sculpted weave. She took her seat opposite Mike.

"Tina needs a lift up to Muswell Hill," Trevor explained, giving Mike a secret wink. "So I said we'd drop her off later. As we're going that way anyway. Tina, this is my friend Mike, Mike Phillips. The one I was telling you about. You know, the one that plays for Arsenal." With a big grin on his face, Trevor flashed another secret wink.

"Arsenal!" Mike exclaimed despite himself.

"Yeah, Arsenal…you know, the football team." Another wink. More obvious this time.

"I don't even support them!"

Chuckling, Trevor turned to Tina. "I told you he's shy didn't I? He doesn't like me telling people that…anyway, like I was telling you, his wife has just left him and he's been feeling really low and lonely, y'know. Tragic story, she uhm left him for a better footballer."

203

"Does she play for Arsenal as well?"

"Please Tina, don't take the piss…this is serious. He really does play for Arsenal."

"How comes I've never seen him then?" Tina asked.

Whatever Trevor imagined, it wasn't going to be so easy to hook Mike Phillips up. Tina didn't seem the least bit interested in him and kept asking him why he talked so posh. And that wasn't a compliment. Mike didn't take a shine to her either and was guilty of looking down his nose at her as she clumsily mixed up her long words and got her grammar wrong. There was nothing to do, but drive her home as promised. She said that it was the first time she had ever been driven in a Rolls Royce and seemed more interested in Trevor than Mike when she discovered that he owned the car. But Trevor didn't need a woman. He was doing all this for Mike's benefit.

"Getting back to the business at hand," Mike began when they had dropped Tina off outside her house in Muswell Hill and the Rolls pulled away again, "how much exactly do you think you want to invest?"

"I can only bring it to you like this, I'll write out a blank cheque if you find me the right shares to buy and you can convince me that I'm not going to lose my money. What I want is a guaranteed profit."

There was no such thing when playing the stock market, Mike insisted. It was like gambling. The only thing you could do was base an investment on the past performances of any company and right now the companies that he had suggested buying shares in were the best past performers, the blue chip companies.

"Blue chip, red chip, black chip…whatever. I don't care what colour the chips are. I just want to make sure I make a profit. And I've got to be certain that I can trust you with that amount of money. I don't allow anyone to get in my business unless I can trust them." He glanced out of the car window. "There's nobody I can really trust out there but myself. Unless you prove me otherwise."

Trevor winked. Mike smiled. He was going to make sure that Trevor trusted him. Especially when he thought of his commission on the blank cheque Mike intended to sign.

"Look, all this talk of business we can leave to work hours. Let me take you on a trip, we can talk business tomorrow, or the day after, or next week. Whenever. Tonight, we're going to party."

Trevor should have said that they were going to 'check gal'. The Rolls pulled up outside a four-storey house in Islington. The chubby white chauffeur climbed out first and opened the rear door for his passengers.

"We'll be here for a couple of hours, Simpson. Wait for us," Trevor said.

The uniformed chauffeur tipped his peaked cap. Trevor put a reassuring arm around Mike as they walked up the garden path.

"You're going to enjoy tonight, Mike. Trust me. You're going to have a good time and it's all on me."

He pressed the intercom.

"Who is it?" a female voice asked.

"It's Mister Loverman," Trevor replied with a grin.

"How you doing baby?" the voice came back. "Where've you been hiding? You're acting like you can't call because you're busy and all that…"

"Lisa baby, just open the door."

The buzzer went and they opened the door, walked in and waited for a moment in the hallway until the door to the ground floor flat was opened by an attractive chocolate-skinned woman in her late twenties wearing a white catsuit. She hugged Trevor briefly.

"Don't think I'm forgiving you," she said. "It's been so long. You've got a phone, use it."

Trevor smiled and turned to Mike.

"This is Lisa. Lisa, Mike. Mike's one of the hottest black stockbrokers in the country."

Lisa smiled alluringly and told them to step right in.

Her flat was elegant. A large two bedroomed ground floor flat on a secluded road in Islington, it was bright and cheerful, with polished wooden floors and a huge white bearskin on the floor. Lisa showed them into the through lounge, where her friend Monica was flicking through the satellite channels. Monica, in her black cat suit, was a browning and looked younger than Lisa. She looked up and smiled when they entered.

"I suppose I'd better do the introductions. Monica, this is Trevor, my ex that I told you about. He's the one with that car company. Very rich. And this is...what did you say his name was...?"

"Mike," Trevor filled in, "and he's one of the most successful black bankers in the country. He's going to be famous and very, very rich."

Mike smiled proudly.

Lisa went to get some more drinks from the kitchen and when everybody had a glass, they sat down talking while the TV flickered in the background.

"I've been looking through all the papers," Lisa said, "but there's nothing special that I want to see. I've seen all the best films and all of the plays advertised for tonight seem like a waste of time. What about you, Monica?"

Monica looked up from watching the TV screen, where C. Riley was shaking his stuff with a new single, *When A Woman Loves A Man*.

"Do you want to go out somewhere tonight?" Lisa repeated.

Monica shrugged her shoulders and said she wasn't bothered. She was hungry though.

"Well we could go out to a restaurant I suppose?" Lisa suggested.

"Why don't we just order some food from a restaurant and we can eat here instead?" Trevor said. "I mean your flat's more comfortable than any restaurant."

"That's up to you, I don't mind. You fine with that, Monica?"

"Sure. As long as we're not sending out for any cheap takeaway."

Trevor assured her that he ate nothing but the best food. Mike said he was happy eating anywhere. He was also feeling a bit hungry. So it was settled then. Trevor dialled Simpson in the car and told him to drive to his favourite Italian restaurant on Upper Street with orders for various types of pasta.

Mike loosened his tie and started a conversation with Monica who was sitting next to him on the sofa.

"So what do you do for a living?" he asked.

"I'm a model," she said, blowing a bubble with her chewing gum until it burst.

"Oh really? What kind of modelling?"

"Oh all kinds," she said.

"Anything I would have seen?"

"Well I'm on the cover of Black And Blue this month."

"I don't think I know that. What kind of magazine is it?"

"A girlie magazine."

"Oh you mean like Cosmopolitan or Vogue?"

Monica looked up at him with a quizzical look. "No silly, girlie magazines…nudes."

Mike cast a critical eye over Monica's well-shaped body, in the figure-hugging cat suit. He had to admit that she did look attractive and he began to wonder what she looked like naked. Nude magazines weren't his thing, but he was going to make a point of buying this month's issue of Black & Blue.

They continued talking and Mike was surprised that he actually found Monica interesting. He never normally found himself attracted to the kind of girl who wears catsuits and chews gum. But that, and her painful cockney-patois speak, aside, she was actually quite intriguing and they hit it off almost immediately. She seemed to enjoy talking as much as Mike enjoyed hearing her talk. She seemed genuinely interested in his work as a stockbroker and soon got around to asking all kinds of questions trying to find out if he lived alone.

That fact alone made her even more attractive to Mike. She was determined to make it in life, but not the hard way. She wanted the fastest route with the greatest results and the least expenditure of energy. That's why she had chosen a profession where the money was easy. And she liked to spend money as easily as she made it, she said almost proudly. Somehow money just seemed to slip through her fingers like running water.

"Easy come, easy go," she smiled at Mike. "There's always a way to make more money."

Mike was impressed by her attitude. If he was looking for a relationship that provided excitement, thrills, mystery, and sensuality, he would probably get involved with Monica. In some ways she was just like him, and in other ways her world provided a welcome contrast to his methodical, boring life.

"I'm looking for that pot of gold at the end of the rainbow also," he told her with a friendly smile. "We're all waiting for that one big break that we can retire on. Then all our troubles will be over. Easier said than done though."

At that point, Trevor reached over and passed Mike a burning fat spliff.

Mike hesitated. He had smoked pot a couple of times when he was a student, but it wasn't his poison and he suspected that it would be a bad idea. He shook his head.

"Let me tell you something," Trevor said, a glazed look on his face. "It's my number one tip on success in business.

If someone offers you something, always accept. This applies particularly to sex and drugs. Never refuse. Smoke your herbs man, it will give you inspiration in business. I'm serious, man. I'm not joking."

Mike took hold of the spliff reluctantly and had a quick puff from it before passing it on to Monica. She held it between her lips seductively and took a slow, long draw. It took twice as long for her to exhale all the smoke in her lungs. She repeated the process, then passed the spliff back to Mike who took a couple of quick puffs and passed it back.

Meanwhile, Trevor was dancing around in the living room, pulling on another spliff and singing out of key:

Drink up de Guinness smoke up de chronic,
Gal start to bawl, me give her de tonic,
Gal get me performance and then get astonish
Run left she draws an' ah tell me she panic
Gal want de lovin' and dem want de romance...

"I love a good spliff," Monica said. "It helps relax me, you know."

Mike nodded. His eyes were bloodshot but he didn't know.

"You know the best way to smoke a spliff...?"

Mike didn't but had the feeling he was about to learn.

"Let me show you," she said and inhaled the remains of the spliff deep in her lungs. Then before Mike realised what was happening she pulled his face towards her until their lips touched and she exhaled into Mike's half-open mouth. The force of the smoke entering his lungs, made Mike cough violently.

"Just relax," Monica urged him. "Try and enjoy it."

Mike coughed some more. He was trying to enjoy it, but this was the strongest spliff he had ever smoked and he began to wonder whether Trevor had laced it with some stronger proscribed drug.

Simpson arrived with the meal a short while later. They were all hungry by now and so it didn't take long to eat the four different types of pasta ordered. There was nothing left when they were finished. Everybody agreed that Mike had eaten the most and teased him about it. Mike didn't care any more. He had removed his tie and jacket and wanted to remove his shirt. He needed to relax. He leaned his head back on the sofa looking wasted. He felt good, though, very horny.

"Me and Lisa are going to check a connection in Brixton," Trevor announced suddenly.

Mike looked up, a moronic expression on his face.

"We'll be about an hour and a half. Don't do anything I wouldn't do," Trevor said with an overstated wink. Mike winked back. "One more thing," Trevor said, pulling out his wallet, "you might need this." He slipped Mike a condom while Monica's attention was on the television. Mike tucked it into his back pocket.

He had barely heard the front door slam, when his arm snaked involuntarily around Monica. She turned to face him and stared hard into his red eyes. Mike stared back and realised for the first time that Monica was not just a pretty face, she was a stunning beauty. He had flutters in the stomach, twinges in the back, and heart palpitations as he considered doing what he really wanted to do. Tonight, the spliff was doing his talking for him and before he knew it, he was asking Monica if they should make themselves more comfortable.

"I feel so great."

"Ready to go all the way?" she asked.

"Yes, all the way."

She accepted his invitation and their affair began that very night.

92% of the men interviewed admitted that they didn't tell their partners regularly enough how much they cared for them. 8% said they did.

SWEET SIXTEEN

Dear Campbell,

How are you? You'll probably be surprised to be getting a letter from me after all these years, but not as surprised as I am that I am finally writing it. Believe me, this is not the first attempt I have made at writing you a letter, but it will be the first one that I succeed in posting.

First, let me thank you for all the cards you've been sending and the cheques that you sent for my daughters. That was very kind of you and I hope that some day they'll have a chance to thank you personally. Meanwhile, the money is in a little account that I opened up at the local bank in their names.

What can I tell you? It's been five years and it feels like I can't say that much about what I've been doing because I haven't done much and most of what I've been doing you already know. You know that I got married and that I moved down here to West Sussex with my husband. You know about the twins who are four years old now. What else is there? Not much. My life is a lot quieter than it was in London. Maybe that's good and maybe it's bad. Either way, it's a fact. You know we all change. I'm not a twenty-five year old wild child any more. I'm almost thirty now and I'm not getting any younger.

Enough about me, how about you? Stella said she bumped into you a while back and you were still driving a Jag, so I presume you're still working for the same cab company. How are things there? I hope you're not working too hard. What have you been up to? Not getting into any more trouble with the police I hope (I heard about your escapades at the Brixton riots five years ago. Mummy told me she had to bail you out). And what about your situation? I suppose you must be married also. Do you have any kids? Boys or girls? What are they like? How old are they?

If you feel like writing, it would be good to hear from you. I love renewing old friendships. Until then, keep the faith.

Yours

Dionne (Phillips)

Reading one of her letters made Campbell feel he was right there with her. It was a chance he had to take...If there was any opportunity, he wanted her in his life.

Dear Dionne,

Even if it took fifty years, I would be just as happy to hear from you. Your letter arrived this morning and I read it before I went to work. It made me smile. Even though you're five years older, I could hear your voice in every word, just as I remembered it. It was funny to read all the things you thought I must have done in the last five years. No, I'm not married. And no, I haven't got any kids. Don't ask me why, that's just the way it's been. A lot of women don't believe me when I tell them. It's like the thought of a black man who is thirty five years old and doesn't have any kids is an improbable one.

It was good to meet your friend Stella, she was full of praise for you and talked about how you've got involved with a lot of things down there in the countryside and that you've made a lot of friends, but that you were the only black family for miles. How do you cope? That's one of the reasons I don't like to go too far out of London. It can't be easy trying to keep a low profile. Stella and my friend Trevor seem to be hitting it off quite well—on a platonic level of course. Now that she's married, it wouldn't do to be otherwise. Don't worry, I can vouch for him, he's an honourable man. Besides he's met her husband who seems to be relaxed with the idea of his wife having male friends with whom she goes to the pictures or to the theatre. That seems like a pretty cool relationship. I hope your relationship is just as cool. When you see a couple like Stella and her husband, you realise that this marriage thing can be pretty cool also. One day, I hope, it will be my turn to meet the right woman and to get it together. I'm looking forward to it.

I hear from your mother that you come down to London sometimes. You ought to give me a call when you're down. We can maybe go out for a coffee or have lunch together. For old times' sake. It would be good to see you again. I'm sure that you haven't changed one bit, despite giving birth to two children.

Give the twins a kiss and a hug from 'uncle' Campbell.

Yours

Campbell Clarke.

Dear Campbell,

It's another sunny day with another bright blue sky. Your letter arrived early this morning. You also sound exactly the same.

How do I cope out here in the countryside? With great difficulty and with the help of a stack of reggae and soul CDs. It hasn't been easy being the only black family, but I feel like a pioneer. In ten years' time, who knows? The whole of West Sussex may be black (joke, that's hardly likely).

I still can't believe that you haven't found the right woman to settle down with and start a family. Still, there's no hurry. I'm sure Miss Right is just around the corner.

I really do hope that your friend Trevor is a gentleman when it comes to Stella. She's one of my oldest friends and I would hate to see another man coming between her and her husband. She waited several years for Lee to come back from America where he was completing his studies, and I know how much she loves him. I wouldn't even want Lee to have any reason to be jealous of her.

That's how a lot of grief starts in relationships. When one person starts getting jealous of the other person it's a recipe for disaster.

Stella's really intelligent. You might think that she's nothing more than a poor little rich girl who spends her time raving and shopping, but she's got a brain and she's using it working on her film scripts. That's where her career is really headed. When she gets one of the major studios to accept one of her scripts you'll see, she'll become a really hot property. I've read every script she's completed, and believe me, they would make some great movies.

The only problem is that they are very much from the black point of view, so I guess that scares a lot of major studios away, but you know what, if they're not interested in that, then she and I will get some money together and make a little movie of our own. That's our plan. We've been talking about it for a long time and pretty soon we'll get round to it. We already have a name for our film company — Stedi Films.

It's unbelievable how time just flies right before your eyes. I still can't believe that it's five years since we've seen each other. I still have a vivid memory of going to see Othello with you. It feels like it was only a year ago. Well, I'll post this letter now so that you can get it before time flies again.

Sincerely
Dionne.

Campbell read her letter and decided that he was going to try and make his dreams come true. He had to get her. He wanted to tell her exactly what his feelings were, but somehow he couldn't find the courage to write down the right words.

Dear Dionne,

I've tossed and turned in my bed all night long and now it's daybreak, I'm tired, exhausted and still have a feeling in my head

215

which feels like a fever. Sleep is out of the question anyway so I got up to write this letter instead.

I told Trevor of your concerns for Stella and he assured me that his intentions were strictly honourable.

Are you still into clothes? As I remember, whenever you were dressed right you could knock 'em dead. Yes, I remember now. You could probably throw anything on yourself and it would look good. Well, I'd love it if you could go shopping for clothes with me whenever you're in London and you've got the time. I've got a bit of money and I've decided to use it on getting an entire new wardrobe. But what do I know about style and fashion? I could do with a woman like you to point me in the right direction.

And are you still into photography? I wouldn't mind some day if you would take a picture of me—I'll pay for it—whenever you're up in London and you've got the time.

You say you still can't quite believe that I'm young, free and single. Well, it's true. I've done a lot of travelling since we last met. I've been around the world, to all the major cities, broadening my mind and learning about different people and their cultures. My travels have taken me places and given me experiences that few others ever have. And I've met many women on my travels, but it's funny, the women that you just want to be friends with all want to be your lovers. And the women you want to be your lovers, they just want to be friends. Isn't that strange? And then when you meet a woman who you could think of as your wife, she ends up being somebody else's wife. Why does life always have to be that complicated? Why don't things ever work out smoothly?

Like this one woman I've been keen on for a while now. She is a fascinating lady with personality and charm, who commands the attention of everyone around her. But somehow she's never noticed me. If only I could express how I really felt, how good she really made me feel. Maybe she would realise that I was the man she had always been looking for. On the other hand maybe it would just piss her off and ruin our friendship. Maybe she just wants to remain friends and nothing more. So I've made the choice that *being her friend is better than not having her at all.*

I spend every day thinking about her. I can't explain what's going on in my mind and why I feel like I do. I just do.

Your mother says you were in London last week. Why didn't you give me a call?

Sincerely
Campbell.

Campbell's latest letter filled Dionne with mixed up thoughts. *Why am I feeling like this?* She wanted to reply to it straight away, but instead took her time. By the next day she started writing, but it took another week before she completed a draft she was satisfied with.

Dear Campbell,

You're not the only one of my friends who have complained that I never stop by to say 'Hi' when I'm in town. But remember, I'm a mother with two kids and it's always such a rush trying to get everything done before I have to get back to collect my babies. I'd like to pick out clothes for you. It will be fun. I miss small things like that in my marriage. You see, my husband doesn't think that shopping for clothes together is important, but the small unimportant things can be the most important things in a relationship.

I hope you won't make that mistake if you get a chance with the lady of your dreams that you wrote about. You should always try to go out shopping for clothes together and tell her what you like to wear and find out what she likes to wear, even if it means erotic undies!

I wish you every success with your lady, I hope she notices you finally. I think you have to find the courage to tell her exactly what your feelings are. You never know, she might feel the same way.

You won't find out until you try. Falling in love is such an easy thing to do, but there's never any guarantee that the one you love is going to love you. However, there's always hope.

I haven't taken photographs in a long time, but when I received your letter, I decided to go up into the attic and pull out the old Nikon camera. I'm sure I can manage a portrait shot of you. Just give me a bit of time and we'll arrange something. I'm really looking forward to seeing you after all this time.

By the way, I was speaking to Stella on the phone earlier today. She said that she was at the cinema with your friend, Trevor. Well, you'll never believe what he told her. He says that he's your business partner and that you're both millionaires. He was joking wasn't he? It's just that Stella doesn't seem to think so. She said that he picked her up in a chauffeur driven Rolls Royce and that he told her about a business you and he have together exporting cars. If this is some big wind-up, please write back and tell me what's going on.

Lots of Love

D

Dear Dionne,

I had the weirdest dream last night, and you were starring in it. I don't know if I should say this, but in the dream, I drove out to your house in the countryside. But when I arrived, I couldn't figure out what I was doing there. I could see you, out in the yard, having a barbecue with your husband and some friends. I could see the twins running around with the other kids. Everybody was laughing and joking and eating and drinking and exchanging pleasantries. The last thing you needed in this convivial atmosphere was for someone like me to come and gate crash, so I remained in the car, across the road from you and simply sat watching, envious of the luck that Mike Phillips had in finding the woman he wanted. I sat there being envious for the next few hours before driving back to London. Then a few days later, we bumped *into each other at Victoria Station, and it was the first time we had met in years and we decided to go shopping together and then afterwards we went back to my place and just kicked back chatting about the old times with a couple of bottles of white wine and an Al Green CD playing softly in the background. We had so much fun that before we knew it it was night-time and you had missed the last train back to West Sussex and you crashed out at my place. Did I tell you that I'm living in a loft apartment overlooking the Thames? If you remember to give me that call whenever you're in London, I'll invite you around.*

Anyway, so you've crashed out in my apartment and that's the part of the dream that I don't remember. But I remember the last part of the dream. It's the next morning, I wake up with my head feeling completely empty, with the sun streaming in through the skylatch and when I turn around, you're lying in the bed next to me. I get up to take a shower and a moment later you joined me, saying that sharing a shower was a good way to save energy.

That was one weird dream, wasn't it?

Millionaire? Me? I can't deny that I've been successful in business, but you know what you're worth on paper isn't the same as you're worth in reality.

Anyway, when it all comes down to it, money isn't everything that they make it out to be. I used to think that being rich would solve all my problems. It doesn't. Once you've tasted caviar and you've drunk champagne, money loses its shine. You need love more than you need money, I realise that now. Because all the money in the world can't get me the woman I want.

Hugs and Kisses

C

Dionne read the letter eagerly, her heart pounding, reading between the lines. She felt something inside so strong for him and had realised that she had always felt something, ever since the first time she saw him. Why had she forced herself not to feel anything for him? Why had she made sure that nothing could happen between them? She suddenly wished she could see Campbell. But if she did that she might never come home. No, the best thing she could do would be to play it cool and not let him know her true feelings.

Dear Campbell,

First, congratulations on your business success. You deserve it.

As for dreams, I don't believe in them any more. That's what marriage does to you. Every woman deserves the man of their dreams, but how can you recognise him when you meet him? BI thought I had found him, so I married him. I loved my husband and showered him with affection, but a fat lot of good it did me. Still, I'm not the first woman who has loved too much and I won't be the last.

The thought of a knight on a white horse is enough to make any red-blooded woman consider throwing over friends, family, and career to follow him wherever he beckons. I know that knight's out there somewhere, I just wished I had married him.

You know, I've kept every letter and card I've ever received from you. They are all tied up in a neat package tucked away in a trunk, where I can get to them easily when I feel the need to become sentimental.

Campbell, I really value your friendship.

Love

D

Campbell's next letter arrived by courier, with a red rose attached to it.

Darling Dionne,

Yet another hazy afternoon. I've got suede loafers on my feet and a baseball cap on my head (I told you I was in SERIOUS need of help with my clothes, when are you coming to London next?) and I don't want to be writing this letter. I would rather put down my pen and just rush on over to you so that we could meet and talk face to face, toe to toe, closely. Maybe even give each other a hug or two. Because Dionne, there's something I must confess: you are the lady of my dreams that I told you about... I'm still crazy about you. After all these years. I know, you're still a married woman. But I've got to let you know that I'm here for you, if you ever need me.

Maybe it's a pity that we've become friends. I can keep playing the friend if you want and pretend that my heart isn't beating away thinking about you, but didn't you know that I wanted to be more than friends, that I had much more on my mind? And it could happen, it really could. All you've got to do is see me in a different light. When we finally get together, you will.

Dionne, I need to hug you up...writing to you is nice, but not nice enough. It would be better to see you face to face. GIMME A CALL!

Thinking about you
C

Naked And Ready

"Watch him nuh, him all ah walk like a champion, talk like a champion…It's looking like my boy is full up ah action. Lock up your daughters dem! 'Cause Sweetbwoy ah come!"

Sweetbwoy acknowledged Bucky's greetings with a little rap of his own.

"What a piece ah body gal tell me where you get it from, knock 'pon your entrance, ram-pa-pa-pam-pam, gal let me in, me have the t'ing wha' you ah wait 'pon…"

It was the first Sunday of the month and Black Man United were enjoying their monthly get-together at the pool. The Red Stripe and Dragon was passed around from one man to the next and there was 'nuff chat and joke.

"Yaow Clarkey!" Trevor called across to his spar. " 'Bout dat gal deh. Wha' she name? Dionne? You don't have to worry 'bout dat no more. I have a feeling everyt'ing gwine turn out copasetic. Seen?"

The rude bwoys were also in the place to be.

"So how much gal you ah go distress tonight, supe?" Mikey asked.

"Personally, I don't deal with dem three-in-a-bed business any more you know, star. I'm into the one-to-one relationships right now."

"Wha'???!!!"

This was some revelation. As far back as people could remember, Sweetbwoy had always had women in abundance. Wasn't he the one who used to say that monogamy was for low budget people?

"I can't believe it myself," Sweetbwoy said. "I never thought one woman could hold me down but believe me, when you find the right woman she can take you places you've never been before, show you worlds other women just couldn't take you to. No man, I'm a changed man. I've found Miss Right."

"So when's the wedding?" Tuffy chirped in.

"Man, I don't want to talk about dem things. It's pure stress. Watcha nuh, the woman won't leave her husband. Cho'! Can you believe she'd rather carry on living with her *maama* man than come shack up with the Sweetbwoy."

There were chuckles from everybody. For once, Sweetbwoy's sweetness hadn't worked its magic. It was refreshing to see that he was mortal like the rest of them.

"And she's an uptown woman as well, you know," Sweetbwoy said. "When I tell you she's criss, I mean *criss*. She ain't no raggamuffin. She's got corn. Lives in a farmhouse out in Sussex."

Campbell reeled from the shock.

"This woman, what's her name?"

"Dionne," Sweetbwoy answered. "You know her?"

Dionne didn't need an excuse to pack up her bags, take her children and abandon her home and marriage. But she got one anyway.

Monica had phoned one morning and explained everything.

"You don't know me, but I know you. I know all about you. Mike's always talking about you. You see, we've been sleeping together for a few months now. It was just a fun thing for me. But things have changed. You see, I'm pregnant. Your husband is the father. But he's trying to get out of his responsibilities. First he tried to talk me into getting rid of it. But I didn't want that. Anyway, it's too late for that now. Oh, he says he'll pay, but he doesn't want to see me or the baby when its born. That's not right. He says that this baby could ruin his marriage. The baby's not even born yet and already it's getting the blame for everything. I just thought that if you could talk to him, you know, make him understand. If you told him that it was okay to see his child, maybe it would help. I'm sorry to have to break it to you like this, but I didn't know what to do. I was desperate, I haven't been able to sleep properly for weeks and that's not good for the baby. I knew you lived in West Sussex, so I went through every Mike Phillips in the phone book, until I got hold of you."

Dionne's things were already packed and waiting in the boot of the Range Rover when Mike came home. He denied it of course. He said that he knew this Monica woman, but it was a case of fatal attraction. "More like foetal attraction," Dionne said, unimpressed. "I should have done this years ago, you bastard." With that final comment she called the children, climbed into the car and drove off.

Dionne checked into the hotel in Bayswater around midday, after leaving the twins with their grandmother in Hampstead for the day, and went immediately up to the room. She popped the door open with her keycard and threw her handbag on the king size bed as she entered. Almost out of habit, she went to the window and checked the view and then went to the bathroom to see that it was clean. Not that she was going to use the bathroom. She didn't intend to be there that long.

She paced up and down nervously. She had thought it through, but she still didn't feel good about it. But she had made her decision and knew what she had to do. She just didn't want to seem like a bitch. She had used Eric when she needed him for her sweetness and now when she no longer required his services, she was going to end it by dumping him. But she couldn't carry on with it. That wasn't what she wanted in her life any more.

She glanced at her watch again. It was a quarter past twelve. He would be there in fifteen minutes. Oh how the hands of time could tick slowly when you were the bearer of bad news. She didn't know how Eric would take it, but she knew after his recent declaration of love that he wasn't going to be overjoyed. How could she tell him how she felt without breaking his heart? It wasn't going to be easy. She herself had been in the same position before and knew how it felt to love someone who didn't love you back and then at the end of it to be told that they didn't need you any more.

She paced up and down the room, glancing at her watch regularly. She thought of the good times with Eric. How he had been her redemption when she was at her lowest ebb, in a marriage with no future. She even smiled despite herself when she thought of how Eric was always full of jokes and able to make her laugh. But she didn't want to think about that. She looked at her watch again. 12.20. She walked to the door nervously and opened it and looked up and down the corridor outside. It was empty, there was no sound from anyone. She went back to pacing up and down the room.

She needed a cigarette. She had so much nervous tension she could barely contain herself. Supposing he took it the wrong way and refused to accept her decision. Why was breaking up so hard to do? The last thing she wanted was a scene with Eric, she really didn't need that now. She didn't want to keep flitting from romance to romance in search of her Prince Charming. She had to tell him what had happened to her, she had to explain everything to him. She had to tell him about Campbell, so that he would understand it wasn't her fault. He had been in her life all this time and now that she knew she was in love with him, she wanted to make something of it.

She was thinking so hard, that she didn't even notice that she had left the room door ajar, nor that a well-dressed black gentleman had entered and was standing watching her. It was the tantalising fragrance which wafted in with him which first alerted her to another presence in the hotel room. Then she saw him out of the corner of her eye and jumped back in surprise.

Dionne didn't recognise him at first. The face looked vaguely familiar. It was a face from the past, from her past, but the Savile Row suit, the Rolex watch and the aura of wealth, seemed unfamiliar.

The man was staring deep into her eyes, the smile on his face slowly broadening. She looked away nervously. *Those eyes, those lips, that smile…*

"Hello Dionne."

At the sound of her name, her eyes lit up with recognition. This was somebody she was longing to see…had longed to see…for so long.

"Campbell?"

He nodded. "It's been a long time."

After so many years, she didn't know exactly how he would feel about her, but when she saw that look in his eyes, she knew.

He felt like lovers do when they have no control. He wanted to kiss her, hug her, hold her. After all that time, he knew, from the moment he saw her, that he was still in love with her.

"But how did you…?"

He held his finger up to his mouth, the look on his face said that he meant business. He turned around and closed the room door. Her heart pounded as she admired him. He looked so elegant. She was surprised that he had even asked her to help him go shopping and pick out some clothes. He seemed to be doing a very good job of being able to sort out

226

clothes for himself without any help. He turned around and came face to face with her again. Looking deep into her eyes, he slowly but surely pulled down her jeans and then lifted up her blouse. He loosened his silk tie and pulled his jacket off, then his shirt, and held his chest warmly against hers, squeezing her gently for the first time. He must have been going down to the gym regularly because a body that good didn't come from sitting in his car.

When you haven't been squeezed for a long time, you look forward to the next time and when the next time comes you hope that it's going to be sweet and hold you through until the next time. Dionne wanted him to keep holding her, keep squeezing her.

It felt so good. She wanted to say something but every time she tried, he lifted a finger up to her lips to hush her. He wasn't going to let any talking spoil it this time. This was the moment he had been waiting for for a long time.

She knew he wanted her, she could see it in his eyes. She wanted to tell him that it was okay, that it was exactly what she wanted also. She wanted to ask him how he had tracked her down, but something told her that she didn't need to ask questions or even warn him that her part-time lover might walk in. Nothing outside the room was important.

She waited in vain for him to say something. She didn't know what was going on in his head and that he was praying so hard that his knees were knocking, his heart was almost leaping out of his mouth and he was quaking in his boots. The confident Campbell Clarke that she had known, was somewhere else at this moment. The man that stood before her was like a boy about to lose his virginity.

Campbell lifted her head up to his, and almost in slow motion, kissed her gently on the lips. His kiss tasted of honey…the sweetest honey. She could feel a tingling in her toes as the kiss became stronger and more passionate. He could feel his heart flutter as he felt the warmth of her tongue dart into his mouth and the comfort of her arms tight around his waist. They stood like that for the next five minutes, before he undressed her *slooowly*.

When they made love, it was like nothing she had ever experienced before. Not in her wildest imagination, had she imagined that making love could be like this. Nothing in creation could compare to what this man did to her. Everything seemed so beautiful. It didn't matter if the sky was grey with clouds, it would look blue to her. She forgot what time it was, what day it was and she didn't want to think about how she would feel tomorrow. *When we've got tonight, who needs tomorrow?* She just knew that she was in heaven. She didn't know what he was doing to her but he was doing it right and she moaned and waited and moaned and waited and dreamt and prayed for him to keep on doing it. For it to go on forever. She would do anything for him, give him anything he wanted as long as he kept giving her some of that good good loving he was giving her. It was pleasure unlike anything she had ever experienced before. The fire that had burned inside her for so long was ablaze and she urged him to take what was his…to take it…take it all. "Yes, yes, yessssss!"

There had been magic in the air all day and all night long. She had called up her mother when she realised that she wasn't going to make it back to collect the kids, and Valerie was only too happy to have her grandchildren spend the night with her, particularly when she heard that her daughter was with Campbell. He had confessed his true feelings for Dionne the last time Valerie had invited him in for a coffee. And although she had wanted to help him in any way she could, he had tactfully urged her to leave well alone. If it was meant to be, it would be.

When she woke up in the hotel room early in the

morning, Dionne was still in that halfway state between dream and reality. In the back of her thoughts, she could hear the birds singing their dawn chorus on the trees outside and a dog somewhere in the distance barking, but she seemed to be floating on air, through a fairy tale wonderland.

When she opened her eyes, Campbell was backing in through the door, carrying their breakfast on a tray.

"Just take it easy, baby," he said softly. "You don't have to get up. Everything's been taken care of."

Dionne smiled sleepily and closed her eyes briefly again before purring, "Mmmmnnn, I can get used to being taken care of."

As well as orange juice, coffee and toast, there was a bowl of corn flakes topped with fresh strawberries and slices of honeydew v melon. It was simple, but it looked like a feast.

"You'll never know just how much I've missed you," he told her as they shared an orange juice from the same glass.

"Neither will you," she retorted. "You will never know how much I've missed you...how much I care...even if you tried."

"Didn't you know my feelings for you?"

"No, how could I have? I figured that you fancied me, but that's not the same thing. I thought you just wanted to get off with me. That that was the level of your affection."

"Why? That was the last thing on my mind. I just wanted to love you. Sure, I had dreamt about sex, but only after I had dreamt of what it would be like to spend the rest of my life with you."

She was studying him closely, wondering if he really meant what he was saying, or whether it was just an infatuation from way back which could never be fulfilled in reality. What did he know about love anyway? What did men know about love? Could they ever really mean what a woman means when she talks of love? A love where the question of commitment doesn't even come into play because there would be no need to think about it?

It is a rare man who finds the perfect mate. Most men are aware of the near impossibility of such a search. As he lay in the king-size bed with his arm around the woman of his dreams, Campbell felt like he was flying over the moon and was prepared to accept Dionne as she was without demanding explanations. His role was to be there for her, cuddle her and to encourage her. It was a role which he would take very seriously.

He felt her hand underneath the sheets, caressing his body gently, all over. It was arousing and, when Campbell looked down, the shape of his erect penis coming up through the sheets greeted him. Dionne giggled and tweaked it playfully. Campbell felt his emotions coming on again and gently, silently and soothingly, he whispered the words he had been wanting to say to her, should have said to her, all those years ago.

"The past is the past. Today is the first day of the rest of our lives. I'm so in love with you…whatever you want to do is alright with me," he said, looking at her sweetly. She smiled back and he could see that she truly warmed from the words. "I want to spend my life with you. Over the last five years I've realised that you are the one I need. I want to be the one who loves you. Forever. The only one."

He promised that he would never be unfaithful. How could he? She was the only woman he wanted…he would ever want. He took her in his arms and looked at her sweetly, sincerely.

"Since I first met you, there's only been you in my life. You're in every breath I take…in every step I make. I'm going to devote my life to you. We've wasted too many years. I want you to get your children and move in with me today." His eyes told her how much he cared and Dionne truly believed that she had finally found her everlasting love.

She warmed to his every word. But he didn't have to say those beautiful things, she was his already, lock, stock and barrel. She could wipe all her tears away now, because Campbell really was her knight in shining armour. This was what she had waited for, Campbell was the man she should have married and would have married if she could have brought herself to allow love to come before circumstance. This was a man she could trust with her life. If only she had known that the soul mate she was forever seeking was right there patiently waiting all the time.

They made love again and again and again and in between they talked about every subject under the sun. They had a lot of catching up to do.

END.

BABY FATHER BY PATRICK AUGUSTUS

"Baby Father…an entertaining look at four black guys on the town who enjoy womanising but suddenly discover the joys of parenthood."
Daily Mirror

BERES and Sonia are the model upwardly mobile professional couple, until the day she walks out of and leaves their seven-year-old daughter behind.
Successful fashion photographer LINVALL'S one night of passion has come back to haunt him just as he enters a new relationship.
Thirtysomething GUSSIE is worried that he'll miss the boat if he doesn't find a woman to have children with soon.
JOHNNY is wondering just how he'll explain to his mother that she's got two grandchildren and two new 'daughters-in-law'…AND TO CAP IT ALL, THE MEN ARE DEMANDING THE SAME RIGHTS OVER THEIR CHILDREN AS THE MOTHERS!

ISBN 1-874509-05-0

BABY FATHER 2 BY PATRICK AUGUSTUS

"Baby Father…an entertaining look at four black guys on the town who enjoy womanising but suddenly discover the joys of parenthood."
Daily Mirror

When JOHNNY finally decides to spend some quality time with his baby son, he is vexed to find that his parental duties have been taken over by his baby mother's new lover.
Thirtysomething BERES discovers that his new wife's baby father isn't too happy about the recent developments in their domestic arrangements either.
LINVALL'S neglected his role as a father for so long that now, when he's called to play dad, he's long forgotten how to do it!
Eligible bachelor GUSSIE yearns to have kids but he still can't find a woman whose 'rateable market value' is as high as his…AND TO CAP IT ALL, THE WOMEN HAVE GOT THEM UNDER MANNERS!

"A superb follow up to the massive hit novel Baby Father."
Paperbacks Reviewed

"Patrick Augustus writes with a voice that is totally unique. He deserves all the success he's had."
The Voice
ISBN 1-874509-15-8